THE AMERICA YOU DIDN'T KNOW

THE AMERICA YOU DIDN'T KNOW

DAVID KISSI

The America You Didn't Know

Copyright 2021 © David Kissi

First Edition 2021

ISBN: 978-1-7376170-2-0

Published by Happy Self Publishing
www.happyselfpublishing.com

HAPPY
SELF PUBLISHING

The memoir of a young immigrant in America.

Prologue

As you will find out, my book is unlike any other. So, certain things I assert may not be something one hears every day. My book is hard-hitting, but it doesn't stereotype. It's fairly balanced, including favorable articles and reflections on the police, Nigeria, the US Government in Vietnam, and Black Americans and Africans on the continent and in North America.

The intent of this book is to educate Americans and foreigners about the Great American promise of equal rights for all. This book is not written for the purpose of presenting stereotypes, but rather it promotes general understanding.

Now, even though this book helps one to examine the White man's world, it also causes one to pause and examine what drives immigrants to America. At some point, an immigrant is forced to look back and wonder if it was all worth it to have come to the America they didn't know.

Another subject that I mention is Nigeria. Even many Nigerians don't want to talk about their country because of kidnapping and crime. But they have the potential one day to be a leading African power. And one way to establish that is to read their history which I have done here in this book. I also have family members who live in Nigeria.

Another thing one should be mindful of is people who try to muzzle other people from expressing their views by labeling them as 'racist'. But this is a book that I think should put aside that stereotyping and invite adult debate over such subjects like Africans on the African continent and Black Americans in North America and the White man's interaction with other races.

There is so much that can be learned. For example, I being African can tell you the reason for Africa's poverty is that the people think negatively. This is because all that they see around them is bad food, bad water, bad hospitals, bad schools, an unhygienic environment, and people dying young. They don't see something better than the degradation they encounter every day in their society. The psychology of poverty is the reason why the African has been left behind. This is something some people especially in the West don't know.

Table of Contents

PART III:
REFLECTIONS AND PERSPECTIVES ON AMERICA

Introduction

This book is not written to raise tension or turmoil. It is not about Black versus White, but rather bringing into the open issues we run into all the time. Now, if anyone thinks I am racist, that person is mistaken. The proof of it is that even though I wasn't born in this country, I have been lucky to have known many, many Whites, including Ted Kennedy, George Bush, Sr., Caesar Chavez, the late Labor Leader, High Court Justice William O. Douglas, and others like Corky Luther, my late friend who was an auto mechanic. I have also known Korean, Vietnamese, and Cambodian individuals, even though they tend to be insular. I befriended and hired so many Hispanics I had to learn Spanish to keep up with them. God gave me the talent of being a great salesman, resilient, and despite the odds, this talent has broken barriers in the White and non-White worlds.

To start with, my story is full of contradictions, twists and turns. Perhaps it reinforces the wisdom of Senate Warner of Virginia that in life, as in business, one shouldn't expect to reach point D from point A right away. In other words, one has to go through a detour to reach his ultimate goals. So, from Ghana, West Africa to the White man's world, I have seen lots of detours, stumbles, and close calls to get to where I am now. In the process there were lots of things about America I didn't know and I am still learning.

PART I

Early Observations Making Adjustments After the White man Left the Colonies

Chapter 1

Where is Ghana?

I was born in Ghana in 1949 in Accra, the country's capital. Ghana was then known as The Gold Coast under British rule. According to the earliest Portuguese and Dutch explorers, there was so much gold in that area, the Atlantic Coast of West Africa, that they named it The Gold Coast, or 'Sika Mpoanoh'.

The key tribe was that of the Akans, then dominated by the Ashantis, whose empire at that time stretched from what is now Ghana to the Ivory Coast, Upper Volta, and Togoland. But during the scramble for Africa in the 1870s, the French took parts of the Ivory Coast, Upper Volta, and Mali. And the Germans took Togoland, which was comprised mainly of the Ewe tribe. The Ewes at that time were allies of the Ashantis. Then after some minor revolts, the British took over The Gold Coast fully in 1908. From then on, through 1957, after intense political activities, the British handed over the country to Prime Minister Kwame Nkrumah and his PPC Party who renamed the country "Ghana" at its independence in 1957.

In the 1950s, my family and I found ourselves in Accra. My father then was a successful Kwahu general trader in Accra. He had several wives. That is how we found ourselves on the coast, even though my mother came from the interior. So, some of my father's 14 surviving children belong to the Accra tribe. My mother, however, was not a full-blooded Accra person. She married my father in Accra because after she had attended a British-run boarding school she couldn't find a job, so she had gone to the capital and married early in life.

According to surviving neighbors in Accra, my mother lived very regally. She had servants who did the cooking and took care of the kids – she never touched anything. Then when I was one year old, one of my aunts accidentally dropped me on my head. After that my mother took direct care of me.

In the early 1950s, when the British were preparing to depart, Ghana was a very beautiful country. The streets were clean, and it had a functioning road and train system, education system and two modern hospitals. The best schools in Africa at that time were in Ghana – Mfantsipm and Achimota. All told, the British left about 5 billion pounds in Ghana foreign reserves, according to the World Bank. This was the Ghana I knew when I was about eight years old.

Chapter 2

What an Akan Extended Family Means

In Africa, an extended family member could be your brother, sister, cousins, aunts, or uncles. Even non-blood relatives could be regarded as your real family, too. They can troop in and out of your house anytime. One is not expected to collect on a loan made to a close relative or you would be regarded as unfriendly. This system discouraged people from saving. This in part is the root cause of poverty the White man doesn't fully understand.

Even though I consider myself westernized, I still support the traditional system of helping others without expecting payment. For example, I have sponsored about 20 extended families to the US at a great cost but never asked for payment. This is because I was once a beneficiary in the same way. Now, the downside of this giveaway is that my retirement will be difficult if I keep giving away money.

Actually, there are several reasons why I am now drafting the family history. For one, it can benefit the younger generation. Also, many in our extended family don't make it a habit to record events in writing, even if they are educated. Then there are others like my half-sisters Tawiah Boahemaa and Akua Antwiwaa who cannot speak English and cannot even read and write in Akan. And as time passes, I am afraid much of our family history will be lost. Also, some of the people whom I initially got associated with in New York in the early 70s are dying out now. This includes John Cheatham, David Sampah, and my one-time German benefactor and his wife.

I was the youngest of my father's 14 children from multiple marriages. I was considered brilliant for my age. As a child, I helped with the housework and disposal of the morning trash. I also had a small garden where I grew peppers, tomatoes, onions and corn. I kept this going until I left for Mfantsipim College in Cape Coast when I was about 16 years old. At that time Mfantsipim and Fourah Bay in Sierra Leone were considered the best colleges in Africa.

Now, a guy who has survived landing on his head and grew up as a fatherless boy and then miraculously gained admission to Mfantsipim can attribute this success to God and rich grand uncles, Isaac Adomako and Nana Adomako.

While I was at Mfantsipim, I heard that our grandmother Nana Dorcas had died of cancer when she wasn't more than 60. Nana Dorcas was the one who raised my mother. She taught my mother her excellent cooking and baking skills when my mother Mary was an adolescent attending Yaa Chia Girls School on Roman Hill in Bompata in Kumasi. At that time Mary, my mother, lived with the Dorcas family at a home located around Jackson Park and Asem Boys School next to Zongo in Kumasi. Zongo then was heavily populated by immigrants from Northern Ghana and Upper Volta (Burkina Faso) and Mali.

Aunt Dorcas had three boys and four girls. The males were Karkari, Charles Kwaku Bona Beckson, and Akwasi Acheampong. Acheampong had glaucoma and went completely blind before he was forty and died of cancer. Karkari was an architect. He lived to be 74. The last-born was Charles Kwaku Bona. He was tall and handsome and once stayed in our household at Asafo, Kumasi. Uncle Osei Kojo was his benefactor. But Uncle Osei Kojo fell on hard times after he lost his job as a bus conductor. He wasn't able to work any longer because he was an alcoholic and his two wives left him. Kwaku Bona then bounced from one household to the next, and this instability in later years made him turn to alcohol, too. He now lives in Connecticut, but I haven't heard from him in over 25 years, despite my persistent efforts. Cousin Bona was a very good friend of mine when we were growing up, and my mother did all that she could for him when he was an orphan.

Now shortly after Nana Dorcas died, her daughter, Awuraa Ama, an airline hostess, died of cancer. Then Awuraa Abenaa married a Nigerian and moved to Nigeria in the early 60s. From a picture my Cousin Bona showed me in 1981, I understand she had several children over there who survive her today. Awuraa Abenaa's daughters did look tall or taller than the average African female, and it appeared they were very beautiful.

Another daughter of Nana Dorcas was Aunt Amy. I believe she was born in 1936. When my mother went to marry my father in Accra, Amy and my mother's junior sister, Aunt

Owuanya, later joined our household in Accra as nannies when I was born in 1949. Owuanya was my nanny.

Shortly after finishing ECM Anglican Elementary School for Girls in Kumasi, Amy got married, moved to Canada, and then moved again with her husband to the UK in the 1960s, where for a while she bunked in with my sister Regina when she was in the UK for further studies. I understand Amy upon her return to Ghana opened her own store and sent Kwaku Bona to the Army. Eventually Amy became very wealthy when she became the mistress of General Acheampong, Ghana's Head of State, even though she was still married to someone else. I understand Acheampong showered her with gifts and cash that enabled Amy to frequently travel abroad and shop at Harrods, an upscale department store in London in the early 1970s.

However, Amy forgot all the good things our mother did for her when Dorcas died. Amy, I understand, had a fall out with Regina over a car deal. Then she suddenly took back a plot of land in Accra she had given to Big Joe, Nana Adomako's eldest son. Amy then went to harass the descendants of some slaves my mother's side of the family once owned. Among them was the late Mame Yaa and some of her family members who lived at Dweso Yard next to the then Labor Department Office in Kumasi.

I recall that in 1981, Amy personally escorted her two sons to the US and enrolled them in colleges here. At that time, it was unheard of, for the expenses were too great. During this visit, she and I had a long phone conversation recalling our early years with her in my father's household in Accra where she was our house maid. Unfortunately, within a 7-year period, her two sons died in the US. Then Jerry

Rawlings, upon returning to office through a military coup in Ghana had General Acheampong executed for his alleged corruption. Rawlings died at age 73 in November 2020.

All of the events above did overwhelm Amy, and she lost her mind. She ran naked on the streets and drove out her maids, including our cousin Katie Nana Kwadwoa Dennis from her Accra household. Amy died of cancer and depression in the mid-1990s. One of her daughters, according to my half-brother Kofi Adjei, once lived in Texas.

Amy's youngest sister Baby, according to family lore, also became very wealthy through real estate investments in Accra in the 70s and 80s. However, at some point she incurred some heavy losses that made her insane, and she committed suicide by drinking poison. And Dorcas' eldest daughter, Aunt Awuraa Afua died of heart ailments in 2006. Her eldest son was Henry Shadowy whose father was a Lebanese Timber Merchant at Ahinsan near Kumasi. This in-law did really like my mother, too. I believe Henry still lives in Germany with his family.

Then there was Nana Tanoah who was one of my mother's aunts with whom we did briefly live in her household at Ejusu Yard after relocating from Accra to Kumasi in 1955. Nana Tanoah was married to Mr. Quason, and when he got bored with her, he went after a younger woman half his age. This generated so much gossip. In any case, Nana Tanoah was a woman of some means and had a cocoa farm. She eventually built her own house at Asikafo Ama Tem, a suburb next to Asafo in Kumasi where we lived. But amidst the construction of this property, Tanoah died of cancer when she was in her 60s. Nana Joseph Adomako was the one who lent the funds to Tanoah's daughter to finish construction of that property. But for some unexplained reason, one Yaw Awuah, a grandson of Nana Tanoah, did not get along with Nana Joseph, even though Nana had arranged admission and scholarship for Awuah to attend Opoku Ware Secondary School where Nana was a trustee.

As a cousin, somehow I got along with this Yaw Awuah. But I didn't really know who he actually was until the summer of 1981 when my spouse and I arranged to visit while in London. We gave him advance notice of our intent to visit, but he intentionally avoided us when we arrived from our London hotel.

However, I had a good friendship with Yaw Awuah's sisters, namely Dora and Yaa Yaa. Dora, years later, immigrated to the Ivory Coast where she died of AIDS. Earlier she had introduced me to her two schoolmates at Yaa Achiaa Elementary School. One was Frances and the other was Nana Ama, a real black and beautiful girl whose family lived in the same house as Yaw Amankwaa, whom my sister Victoria later married. Nana Ama then introduced me to her brothers, namely Ata Kora and Johnny, the tall guy. Dora also had another schoolmate known as Theresa Nana Ama Asomoah, who coincidentally was our landlord Wofa Yaw's daughter. Theresa and her parents really did like me, but my mother's anxiety over her serious involvement with me subsided when Theresa married early in 1969 to a wealthy businessman from the Ivory Coast. They had one girl called Bebe and then separated. Then in the mid-70s, Theresa and her half-brother Kwabena Amoah both immigrated to Paris, France. Later she settled in Germany with Bebe and her 8 grandkids. In fact, her parents and elder sister Faustina were beneficiaries of my yearly remittances to Ghana for a long time.

Unfortunately, the landlord and his family's lives ended badly, for they almost all died within a 10-year period. Yaa Ghana and Kofi "Boat" Boateng are the sole survivors, and they now live in Vancouver, Canada.

I also recall that our mother Mary had several other cousins who all, at one time or the other, lived in the extended family household at Fanti Newtown. This included Aunt Dinah Gyembibi, who was very enterprising. After her second husband died, she started her own business and imported high-end clothing, textiles, and watches to Ghana from Liberia. In this regard, Uncle Sarpong and Aunt Owuoanya, who were then residing in Monrovia, helped Dinah by connecting her to big Liberian businessmen who extended credit to her. Sarpong and his Liberian partners had a lucrative Timber Concession. Three of Aunt Dinah's children are Kwaku Hagi, the eldest; Paul Gyembibi, the youngest, both now living in Connecticut; and their sister Naa Serwaa, now a widow who lives in New Jersey. Dinah's second son, Henry, who once lived in Connecticut, has since returned to Ghana. Aunt Dinah died in 1984 or 1985. I understand she was returning from a funeral when her car had an accident, and she bled to death, for there was no ambulance readily available to transport her to the nearest hospital.

Aunt Dinah's blood brothers were Uncle Bonsu and Uncle Kwame. Uncle Kwame was the tallest of all my uncles. He was about 6'8", and he worked as a court clerk at the courthouse then located north of Adum in Kumasi. He had two wives. One was an Ashanti and the other a Mfanti. He and Bonsu also died of cancer as my mother's three brothers did. Dinah's sister Ohiafrewo was about 80 years old when she died. But her youngest sister Aunt Dankwah died at age 29. Her daughter Gifty is now a professional nurse in New Jersey. Aunt Dinah and Uncle Bonsu were very good friends of our mother. Bonsu's half-brother Mr. Appewo now lives in Brooklyn, New York. Wafa Coach was another Uncle who worked for the Post Office in Kumasi. His niece is Comfort Akua Achiaa Owusu who now lives in New Jersey. She was once married to Anue Cofie, a great soccer player who played for Ashanti Kotoko in Kumasi, the Ghana National Soccer Team, and later on for the New York Cosmos in the early 70s. He is now about 70, and he is suffering from dementia. He resides in a New Jersey nursing home in West Orange.

Then there was one Mame Ataa Boateng, a far distant cousin of our Mother. That family in the 60s lived by the Asafo market next door to Adom Fie, a group of Fantis our mother had known since she was a little girl. I recall Mame Ataa's mother was about 50 years old when I was about 10 years, and we occasionally visited them. Mame Ataa's sister was the mother of Georgina and Georgette, the twin sisters. They were very beautiful. Their father was Lebanese. Georgina died of cancer when she was in her 30s. And at one time Cousin Charles Kwaku Bona, Amy's youngest brother lived with Georgette and her Lebanese husband. But Charles left because he reported he couldn't get along with the husband.

THE ADOMAKOS

Nana Kojo Aboagye Adomako, aka Joseph Adomako, and his brother Isaac's parents or parent were related to our great grandparents. According to my mother, they all once lived at the family's ancestral village at Atwima Yabi in Ashanti and later in Fanti Newtown in Kumasi. Nana Joseph might have been born in the early 1900s shortly after the

Yaa Asantewaa's rebellion against British rule. As a young man, Nana Joseph worked for the British conglomerate, the UAC, and early on the company promoted him for his good bookkeeping skills, overall honesty, and his love for God which he found in the Catholic Church. At some point, he took an early retirement and went to work for himself as a beer and beverage wholesaler.

Nana Joseph's dear wife was Mame Nkrumah. She hailed from Bekwai in Ashanti. Out of their seven children, four still survive them.

Nana Joseph was an unusual African in his generation in the sense that he disliked polygamy. Also unusual about him was that he preferred a balanced diet and stayed away from starchy food. This may explain why he lived into his eighties. But phlebitis bothered his right leg when he was in his 60s, and in 1983 he died of prostate cancer. I really do miss him since he was my substitute father.

I do not think Nana Joseph ever met my father, even though Nana had done business earlier among the Fantis in Southern Ghana before eventually returning to Kumasi to run his beer and alcohol wholesaling business. In addition, Joseph had a cocoa farm.

When we relocated to Kumasi from Accra in 1955, we used to visit him at Asafo about a mile from my mother's residence. Nana took an early interest in our education and my mother's welfare. For example, when Mr. Aidoo, the man my mother married in 1956, misbehaved by not providing for the children he had with my mother, Nana Joseph hired a lawyer and took Mr. Aidoo to court for desertion and sought relief in the form of child support for my mother. The court ruled favorably for my mother.

In tandem with the above, Nana Joseph persuaded his junior brother Isaac to secure Cocoa Marketing Board scholarships for our high school education.

At that time, Nana Isaac was very influential, for he was a Member of Parliament in the post-colonial government under Osagyefo Kwame Nkrumah who was the President at the time. As a young man, Nana Isaac was a teacher who rose to become a School Inspector. This high position brought him in contact with various school principals, and that connection landed me a slot with a full scholarship at Mfantsipim, which in those days was one of the most prestigious institutions of learning in Africa.

However, Nana Isaac, unlike Nana Joseph, had two wives. He and his senior wife in the 1960s lived at Kwadoso, a suburb of Kumasi. His senior son became a medical doctor, and in the 80s he moved to Saudi Arabia. Nana Isaac's second wife, Aka Osei Kojo's mother, at one time lived at Adum on a hilly spot next to the British Council. Across the street from them was the Presbyterian Church. She was a day nursery teacher. The nursery was located in Fanti Newtown close to the Kumasi Railroad Terminal. Occasionally I visited both wives, but Nana Isaac was much closer to my sister Regina Awuraa Akosua because she was older and perhaps understood Nana better. I believe at least two of Nana Isaac's sons now reside in Reston, Virginia with their families. Their sister died here about 20 years ago. Nana Isaac died in 1985 soon after Nana Joseph's death in 1983.

Looking back, it was God's act that led Nana Joseph and Nana Isaac to help us. Their cousin Kwaku Mensah, whom my Mother had looked to for financial help because he was once my father's business partner in the 1940s in Accra, ignored us when we relocated to Kumasi in 1955. In fact, until I was 18 years old, I saw him only twice. Then in 1969, he returned from exile in the Ivory Coast after Nkrumah was overthrown by the Army.

Again, we will remain forever grateful to Nana Joseph and Isaac for their kindness. We are also grateful to Nana Joseph's son, lawyer Augustine Adomako aka Nana Yam, the official spokesman or "Ocheaminn" of the Asantehene, aka King of the Ashantis. Now and then he would prep and coach a relative I was sponsoring to come to the US, on what to say or not do in securing US visas.

Now, out of the three branches of our extended families, the Adomakos have the longest lifespans, despite being plagued mainly by asthma.

Chapter 3

Post-Accra 1950

In 1950 life was very tough because when my father died without a will, the local African tradition permitted his sister to seize all his assets. This included his general store near Makola Market in Accra and five plots of land. My father had been wealthy as a general merchant in British Colonial Africa. But we still wonder if he had lived whether he would have been able to maintain that wealth because he had 14 children with three women.

In any case, during my father's lifetime he had underwritten the cost of building and cultivating a large cocoa farm for the benefit of my mother's mother, or my father's mother-in-law, Akua Yeboah. But when my grandmother died, one of my uncles took over the farm to work on it as a supervisor. He eventually took all the revenue and gave us none to support ourselves in boarding schools. The only income we had was from my mother baking bakery products and selling off gold bars my father had gifted to her when they first married. I contributed towards the upkeep of the household by selling bakery products, too. My mother coached me on how to sell, and every morning she would pat me on the back before sending me out, encouraging me not to give up easily. I am still a salesman after all these years.

For a while, my mother's side of the family and my father's sister continued to play games with us. But there wasn't much us kids could do because Nana Kwaku Mensah, who was our father's business partner, had fled to the Ivory Coast because of his political activities. He was the big man that I and my sisters were counting on. Fortunately, on my 15th birthday things remarkably changed, for my mother's grand uncle Nana Adomako Joseph, a cocoa farmer and liquor entrepreneur, and his brother Isaac, upon hearing of our financial predicament, decided to underwrite our school cost plus room and board. They gave us the best education then available in Ghana. For example, Grandfather Isaac Adomako got me enrolled at Mfantsipim where I learned Latin and Greek. It was the best school in Africa then. My sister Vic went to a Teacher's College, and my senior sister Regina was sent to Yaa Asantewaa Girl's School in Kumasi. Later Regina went to Liberia and then to England to finish her education. She died in 2008 and was survived by four boys and her husband George.

Then at the age of 18 the Adomakos, my two grandfathers and my mother suggested I should come to the US. This is because the AID, State Department, Newsweek, and the Peace Corps had a big propaganda machine going that suggested America was the best place in the world to get an education and that everyone was happy in this Paradise. My mother also thought it was a good place to come to because after getting my advanced education I could help my sisters. My mother didn't know anything about the United States. She knew more about Britain through conversing with neighbors and her cousins Aunt Amy who once lived in the UK and Aunt Awuraa Abenaa, an airline stewardess. Mum was forced to marry my father at a young age since she couldn't find a job after graduation. That wasn't something she wanted her daughters to go through.

MEMORIES WHILE GROWING UP IN AFRICA

Looking back, my sisters and I should have made a living in farming. Cocoa farming is the largest occupation in West Africa. Two-thirds of the government's revenue in the Ivory Coast and Ghana are derived from cocoa farming. Nigeria derives 40% of its GDP from farming and 60% of employment is associated with farming.[1] Ironically, an African with some education does shun farming. He would prefer to work in an office in a white shirt and tie rather than to work with his hands. This is the net effect of colonial rule. And this rule has endured long after the White man's presence.

But I did not know this was a direct opposite of what the White man in the West does. Years later, I recall that my German boss, a millionaire, would pick up a broom early in the morning when he arrived at work and sweep the sidewalk of his store on the east side of Manhattan. I sometimes wanted to grab the broom from him and do the sweeping. I did not know that is how the White entrepreneur gets ahead by doing things for himself such that he becomes independent and wealthy.

---

1 See Financial Times dated October 22, 2020-FT Special Report: "African Farming & the World".

DR. NICHOLAS' INFLUENCE

Perhaps the professor who did influence me very highly when I was growing up in Ghana was Paa Nicholas. Dr. Nicholas hailed from British Guinea or Guyana and when I met him at the campus of Mfantsipim in the 1960's he and his mulatto wife had roamed through the whole world until Kwame Nkrumah, the first President of Ghana gave them a refuge and teaching professorship in Ghana.

Paa Nicho was outspoken and that is why perhaps he claims the CIA came after him. The 60s was a hot period of student's activism and that provided a fertile ground for Dr. Nicholas' ideas. He spoke in support of Castro, Che Guevara, Nkrumah, Lenin, Lumumba, and the Red Indian.

A group of about 3-5 students usually met him in his living room on Saturdays and his lectures did run from one to two hours. He taught us how to effectively debate and allowed us to use his private library. This was unheard of for we did not have access to a private library.

Dr. Nicholas was the source of my knowledge about African and Western Civilization and racism, the American economy, Karl Marx, and especially Socialism. Unfortunately, when the Army of Ghana overthrew President Nkrumah, the CIA allegedly engineered to have Dr. Nicholas booted out of Ghana in 1968.

Then 10 years ago, I was reading an obituary in The New York Times, and I read Nicholas had turned up in Guyana and became the Prime Minister of that country. It appeared he had overturned all what he stood for when I met him on Ghana, i.e., he was no more an anti-Capitalist and became a friend of the United States. I do not know what happened to his wife, but both were a formidable team and Ghana did benefit from their knowledge.

MEDICINE IN AFRICA

Triple bypass surgeries, heart transplants, X-ray equipment and ventilators are still very rare in Africa as they were when I was growing up. My sisters were the ones who went to the White man's hospital and clinics where nurses attended to them. I hardly joined them, for my mother made me visit two Juju men. One came from a fierce tribe in Dahomey, and the other was an Ashanti. And if my ailment was whooping cough, one would mix pieces of wood and herb and drink for relief. Agya Yaw from Ashanti was the one who taught me to be fearless in front of wild dogs and deer as well as how to fight off big snakes and reptiles. At some point in my youth, I was so advanced in native medicine that I could mix and apply herbs to soothe a snake bite and cure stomach and chest pains. But my knowledge did not help me much when Kwasi, our Nfanti boy neighbor threw a large stone at me and smashed a toe on my right foot. However, my mother consulted the juju man to cure me and after about a month the broken bone was healed.

In the 60s, there were no insurance policies to take care of ailments, or women for childbirth, or old people having heart attacks. I don't even recall whether anyone had insurance, even though the Guardian Insurance Company of the UK did business with expats and with the Government of Ghana during that time.

Before the British left, they built the Komofo Anokye Hospital in Kumasi for the public. Medical services were free. Prior to that the British had also built a similar hospital in Accra where my senior sister, according to my mother, was born.

In those days, there were also no social security programs or pharmacies to get prescriptions refilled. For those services, one would contact a relative either in Liberia or Britain for help if a hospital had run short.

But when one comes to the US and sees hospitals like Beth Israel, Jamaica Hospital, or Lennox Hospital, and that in some of these hospitals one needs insurance or else he can't get in, many foreign-born are baffled. Fortunately, the emergency room door is always open at no cost. But this explains the high death rates of Africans and Hispanics in the US — they don't go to the hospital right away, since healthcare costs without insurance subsidy is very expensive to them. For example, in New York a woman with breast cancer who spends 5 days in the hospital will readily incur a bill of $15,000 - $20,000 or more. Prostate surgery could easily cost about $20,000.[2] These are some of the things about America many foreigners don't know.

Another event I still recall is that in Africa when a family has a child, there is so much enjoyment. And after about 4 weeks, the child is given a name and all the villagers and family members greet the child with food and gifts of all kinds. The woman doesn't take time off from work, whether she is working on a farm or in a government office. She simply becomes a homemaker all over again. And her husband or family members will take care of her. But since there isn't much good medical care, many African children die early from childbirth. According to the World Health Organization, there is a high rate of maternity deaths in Africa.[3]

---

2 See New York Times October 8, 2020.
3 World Health Organization, UNICEF, United Nations Population Fund and The World Bank, *Trends in Maternal Mortality: 2000 to*

THE PEACE CORPS[4]

Initially, the Peace Corps' objective pursuant to President JFK was to bring American culture and influence to Africa and other places in the developing world. In 1963-1964, there were Peace Corps workers all over Ghana. They taught Math, Biology, and Physics.

Fortunately, since the Soviets were doing something similar, it made the Peace Corps a very important tool of US foreign policy in the developing world. Years later when the African natives or their governments prayed to the US government to expand the limits of what they were doing, the American government brought in a brand new Peace Corps group who could dig wells, assist in medical duties, and increase the production of rice.

The 1960s was a very exciting period in the Peace Corps' history in Africa. Its workers learned to dance to African tunes and Africans learned to dance to American tunes from Louis Armstrong, James Brown, and others. The Peace Corps also promoted sports or events between the US and Ghana or between the US and Nigeria. This made everyone happy. It resulted in the US granting scholarships to young African students to come and study medicine in the US. Conversely, I have a brother who gained a scholarship from the Soviets to attend medical school at LaMumba University in Moscow. But the Soviet's version of the Peace Corps wasn't too popular because of language barriers and the power of American propaganda.

2017 WHO, Geneva, 2019.
4 See New York Times, October 4, 2020, p.4

PART II

Coming to America

Chapter 4

Our Good Neighbor Nigeria

It is hard to discuss Ghana without mentioning that Nigeria is next door. This is because Ghana and Nigeria are essentially the same culturally, except Nigeria has more languages and a larger population. But their DNA, food they eat, and customs are virtually Ghanaian. Nigeria, like Ghana, was colonized by the British, but since this was the tail-end of the scramble for Africa, the British did not do a good job of bringing together all the major tribes to form a nation with a solid base. For example, Nigeria today is comprised of the Ibo in the east, the Yoruba to the west, and the Hausa Fulani to the north. In fact, the current President, Mr. Buhari, is a Fulani from the north. But each one of them is a nation by itself that was thrown together to form the National Federation of Nigeria. And that may explain 10 coup-d'états and the big Biafra War from 1968-1994, which created so much tension between the Hausa, Yorubas, and Ibos.

Nigeria's chief export is oil, and according to estimates, it has been earning roughly $25 billion per year. However, the nation hasn't got much to show for all that money because of corruption. But the average Nigerians should be given credit because they are hardworking and entrepreneurial. For example, if one were to walk down the street in Harlem, New York and see a dentist office shingle from Dr. Earlene Nzoom, one can safely assume it is a Nigerian female dentist. Apart from West Indian women, it is likely you won't see a Ghanaian or Liberian woman who will venture out on such enterprise. And their chief export is its educated class, because most Nigerians, about half of the men, have college degrees, which motivates them to go to almost every country of the world to teach or work.

Dr. Namadzi Azikwe was the first president of Nigeria, and according to Ghana's first president, Kwame Nkrumah, he learned quite a lot from Dr. Azikwe, who was well-known for his academic studies. He taught Nkrumah politics. Among the contemporaries of Dr. Azikwe are Chief Awalowo, the then Chief Minister of Western-Yoruba and Tafa Balewa. Tafa Balewa was a well-known Hausa, and he became the first Prime Minister of Nigeria. Unfortunately, he didn't last long because he was killed in a coup d'état in the 1960s. Then there was General Ojukwu who led his people, the Ebos, into a disastrous secession with the rest of Nigeria and about 3 million died. There are other famous Nigerians like Wole Soyinka who earned the Nobel Prize of English Literature, Chinua Achebe, and Fela Kuti, who was a well-known entertainer in Europe and West Africa. He was a good Ambassador for Nigeria. Also worth mentioning is Dick Tiger, a well-known boxer, who once lived in New York. Now, during the Biafra Civil War, he left New York to visit his family, but he never came back. The assumption was that someone killed him.

In any case, friction between Nigeria/Ghana that had remained hidden like a family tension erupted into the open when Dr. Kofi Busia expelled en masse all Nigerians living in Ghana between 1968 to1970. This brought a lot of inconvenience to Nigerians then living in Ghana, because many had bought or built homes and had children and grandchildren bearing Ghanaian names. A couple of years later, the Nigerians hit back and expelled all Ghanaians from Nigeria. According to unconfirmed reports, they also killed many Ghanaians.

Generally, contemporary Nigerians are peaceful. And there are about 100,000 living in North America. Apart from the occasional accusation of scams, many college-educated Nigerians prefer white collar jobs or drive taxis in the big American cities of Boston, New York, and Chicago.

One thing I noticed about my Nigerian schoolmates and colleagues in the US is that they are not too friendly. And this unsociable demeanor may explain why foreign visitors to Africa don't go to Nigeria. In addition, most of their friendships are here today but gone tomorrow. In fact, to outsiders Ghanaians are friendlier, and that is why Ghana attracts more foreign tourists than Nigeria.

Thus, I have inserted this profile on Nigeria because I have extended family in both Nigeria and Ghana, and we all share similar characteristics. And in reviewing this memoir, this explanation will make it easier for the reader who doesn't know much about West Africa. In other words, it's important to understand that Ghana and Nigeria are almost the same and that we interact with each other daily

— especially someone like me, who has family members in both Ghana and Nigeria. In fact, people ask me all the time whether I am a Nigerian. I am not Nigerian and have never been there. In any case, I used to interpret this question to mean there is a shortage perhaps of men in Nigeria, for this inquiry often came from women.

Chapter 5

A Foreigner's First Impression of America

The main port of entry for most foreigners in the early 70s was New York before Newark Liberty and Miami expanded. It was so exciting to see people from every part of the world in New York, namely Mongolians, Russians, Jews, Pakistanis, Arabs, Nigerian women with huge head gear, Spanish, Black Americans, and Whites.

Initially, the police weren't anywhere to be found unless someone pointed them out to you. This is because the police we had back home or in London were much different and didn't dress as inconspicuously as American police. So, a foreigner gazing at the tall buildings in Manhattan may miss an American policeman standing by. There were restaurants everywhere but if one could not pronounce words on a menu, he simply hid his ignorance by buying chicken.

At that time, the Africans had no churches, so their social outing was usually drinking liquor, beer, and attending each other's parties at their homes on the weekends. Laughingly, most of the Africans who had declared on their visa applications that they were coming here to attend school quickly dropped out and resorted to driving taxis. Virtually none had his own business then like the Spanish, Italians, and the guys in Chinatown and the Bronx. Later, as foreign immigrants started making friends with their American counterparts, many of them were able to find better jobs in schools and colleges.

Unlike the men, the African or foreign women somehow found jobs as cooks, nannies, and nurse's aides relatively fast. Many had language problems, obviously a carryover from Africa, and as usual many had larger families than American women. In the summer, the men played soccer. For a while, the Ghanaians had the best soccer team among other foreigners in New York.

I saw none who went to Broadway shows, but it seems many immigrants had heard about Harlem and its Apollo Theater and had also heard about the Abyssinia Baptist Church then run by Congressman Adam Clayton Powell. It also appeared that many of the immigrants had heard that James Baldwin had grown up in Harlem, and Zora Hurston, Langston Hughes, Maya Angelou, and Adam Clayton Powell all once lived in Harlem, too. The early 70s, and as I understand it the 60s, too, were a really exciting time in New York, especially Harlem.

Until the 1980s, most of the Africans one might have seen on the streets of New York were educated in either the British or French systems of education. Not many modern technical skills were taught, rather it was a continuation of a 100-year-old curriculum where boys like me were taught

Greek and Latin and the women mastered raising babies, cooking, and home economics. On the whole, the colonial masters did not put much emphasis on developing the technical skills of the African natives. They were mainly interested in mining our gold at Obuasi, Ghana; crude oil from Nigeria; iron ore in Guinea; and cocoa farming. This system of neglect prevailed after independence such that as of today many of the commodities shipped to Europe are still in raw form, which is not very profitable.

It's therefore logical that the Africans coming to America or Europe post- independence would not have many technical skills, like operating computers, cash registers, and x-ray machines in hospitals. I remember it was thought to be demeaning for an educated African woman to work on a farm. This too was a carryover from the colonial period when, it's argued, the women without brains had to work with their hands. This wasn't universally true, for my mother had attended a Methodist Girls Boarding School run by British missionaries in the 1940s, and she knew how to type. With that said, she never went downtown to look for work, for she was a baker. Also, boys should have been taught how to operate NCR and Univac systems and Remington typewriters, which were in Ghana. Or, they could have been trained as mechanics who could operate in factories. All this could have contributed to our quantum leap forward to 21st Century economic stability.

But the reality was that, in the new world of America, the African men drove taxis in New York, and some worked in factories in Ohio and Worcester. Many worked as school teachers, and some even continue to as late as today. But it's unusual to see African men operating their own construction businesses as the Spanish did. This is because they hated the idea of working with their hands. As already explained, this is a residual link to a colonial mentality.[5]

So, somewhere in 1970 or 1971, I arrived in America and stayed with my cousin who had arrived earlier. Her husband was playing professional soccer with the New York Cosmos. My cousin and brother-in-law found a job for me with a sporting goods company run by a German family in New York. At that time, the family had lost a son and the other son was on his way to Vietnam after joining the Navy. At the last moment, the Navy discharged him on grounds of disability, and he came home. In his absence, however, I became like the lost son of my boss' wife, and I went everywhere with her. She showed me a variety of American dishes in restaurants and also canned food in supermarkets. Initially, it had been difficult to understand how to read a menu in a restaurant.

After staying with them for about two years, I had to follow my mother's instruction to pursue higher education as soon as I could. So, I enrolled in school at Husson College in Maine. Another reason why I returned to college was because in those days a foreign student was required by immigration law to report to immigration authorities within one or two years of being in the US. It turned out that 1973 was a good year, for the US government accepted my visa renewal bid. In addition, while the war in Vietnam was winding down, the Selective Service also ruled I wasn't immediately available for military service because of my enrollment in college. When I left New York for Maine, I had $12,000 - $15,000 saved. Part of the lot was from savings,

---

5 See New York Times September 23, 2020, "Report Links U.K. Treasures to Colonialism and Slavery" by Elian Peltier.

and the other portion came in the form of gifts my boss' wife gave me now and then.

All told I had my post-graduate degree at Northeastern University and the University of Maryland, College Park when I was about 30 years old.

Chapter 6

Heading North to New England

As mentioned, newly arrived foreign students were required by a provision in the US immigration law at the time that said foreign students should renew their visas yearly or every three years. So, I had headed north to Maine in 1973 to enroll in school.

But another reason was that I had a friend, Sheryl, whose daughter was killed by her ex-boyfriend, and at that time she asked me to put together a brief from sources she had gathered about her case, including the government case, her writings, and research she had gathered from the neighborhood grapevine. I then summarized the key points of what was at issue, bound it all and Xeroxed a copy on my boss' copy machine. Well, my first attempt at law was successful, for the Brooklyn prosecutor used that as a basis to have Ron, the culprit, after a plea, sent to jail for about nine years.

Now, from the time this two-year-old girl died until the time her alleged killer went to jail, the police now and then came around to talk to the people my friend Sheryl used to hang around with in Brooklyn, the Bronx, and Manhattan, where Sheryl's mother lived. The police cleared me of any wrongdoing, but they were puzzled on how I could prepare a brief for the prosecutor's case with my engaging accent.

So, I stayed at Husson College in Bangor, Maine for about 6 months, or two semesters, through the winter of 1973. I found the landscape of Maine to be really beautiful. Now, while it heavily snowed, I ate all the food I could eat and I made use of the school's large gym. At that time, the number of foreign students at the campus numbered not more than ten. Five of them came from Nigeria, two were from Ghana (including me), and another three were from Asia. On Friday evenings we would drive to the University of Maine at Orono, a far bigger campus where there were many White American female students.

I recall Husson College had a large Black American population. The men mostly came from Brooklyn and Upstate New York. The women came from New Jersey and Philadelphia. I still remember Stephanie White of Patterson, New Jersey. She was the prettiest girl I had ever seen. Since we said goodbye to each other, I have not been able to see her again.

Then summer of 1973 arrived and my German boss' wife, Dorothy, sent word that I should return to New York City, for that is where I belonged. She added that the Catskills, the family's second home, was warm and beautiful, and I could get all the apples I wanted. She had also reserved a job for me at her husband's Soccer Sports store on 1st Avenue on the east side of Manhattan.

Now, before I returned to New York, I had to explain to my Nigerian college friends that returning to the Big Apple was a top priority. What had happened in my time in Maine was that I had run into five Nigerian brothers who had offered to move me to Chicago at the end of summer school.

But Rubenstein, a Jewish friend of mine, counseled against this, and he offered to drive me back to my German family in New York. He prevailed in counseling on this matter because I trusted him. Also, I was impressed with his knowledge of financial markets like the stock market. I had even made money from taking his advice in the past. The market was something no African at that time had ever heard about.

I later saw that the Afro-American students from Brooklyn did not like Barry Rubenstein, and they warned me to watch him. But this was a senseless attack on Rubenstein, for he did like Blacks.

Once on the way to New York, I stopped at his father's home in W. Orange, which at that time was an all-White township. East Orange was all Black. Sometime in 1975, Rubenstein wrote to inform me that he had moved and was now living in a kibbutz in Israel. He wanted me and my family to come and visit him any time. Unfortunately, our correspondence died out, for in 1975 when I moved to Worcester, Massachusetts for further education I left behind the box that held all my mail.

New York always fascinated me, for every tribe on earth, their strange food, smells, clothing that could not be found elsewhere — it could all be found in New York City. This is something I had not realized about New York before coming to America.

From my street corner observation, I think there are more Irish in New York than in Massachusetts. Some of our neighbors were Irish, and I found the Irish in south Boston quite interesting and friendly. I set out to learn more about them, for it's a great feat to be squeezed by the British, survive a famine, and still proceed to America.

Today many big city policemen and firefighters, especially in New York and Boston, are of Irish descent.

The Irish were not the first White immigrants from Europe to come here. They came after the English and Germans. Since they were poor and had few skills, they often worked more as bondsmen or indentured servants and later on ran Union shops in Massachusetts. Apart from singing and storytelling, the Irish did not excel right away. And in modern times, when tribal distinctions are melting away, the Irish are still identified as saloon keepers, policemen, and firefighters in New York, Philadelphia, and Boston. There are some Irishmen who have made advances through the ranks in the US Army and the local police. I understand American institutions prefer to hire FBI and firefighters of Irish descent because they are thought to be 'Yes Men'. This is something I did not know before I came to America.

So back to New York in the summer of 1973, I stayed with my German Boss and his wife during the week, and on the weekends, if we did not go to the Catskills, I cruised around Harlem. Prior to Harlem, I had never seen so many Blacks hemmed in as was seen on the little island of Manhattan. My friend Lillian McMcIllwain introduced me to her sisters

Charlene and Michelle whose mother lived next door to them in Lenox. They thought that if I hadn't seen the Apollo, then I hadn't really seen New York. Unfortunately, on the night we went to the Apollo I was drunk, and I still don't remember which band was playing.

There were also occasions that the African immigrant expats and diplomats would throw big parties with so much booze. There were parties for every excuse imaginable, like parties for heading outdoors, when the Africans named their children, funeral parties, and marriages. The biggest party of all in New York was on March 6th, Ghana's Independence Day. At that time, there weren't more than 200 Africans in all of New York City. Today there are about 2,000,000 combined.[6]

MALCOLM X

There had been so much excitement about Malcolm, the Black National Leader, and his nationalist preachings in the 60s. Though he died in 1967 when he was allegedly gunned down by his fellow Muslims, the early 70s were still characterized with so much frenzy surrounding him, his ideas, and his death. The Muslims as a group broke into three or four factions and kept the drums going after Malcolm died. Much had been written earlier, but it remains a mysterious group, and many Whites looked at their names and lifestyle choices as strange. His preachings preceded him and were mostly about cleanliness, decent homes, abstention from alcohol and pork, and entrepreneurship. These were some of the values that attracted poor and middle-class Blacks to the group.

---

6 See https://en.wikipedia.org/wiki/Demographics_of_New_York_City#Ethnicities_and_enclaves

But the group's internal weakness inhibited its growth. For example, they were not politically active even at the local level where they could have promoted candidates to run for office. This, in turn, could have helped the group to get financial assistance from the government and support their schools. The Muslims also stayed away from state and national politics. And all decisions came from their headquarters in Chicago. That proved its weakness.

When alive, Malcolm broadcasted the plight of Black Americans abroad, toured the Mideast, and came to Ghana, then went to Britain, but the French government barred him from France. He personally achieved much, and even though he had no formal education, he became very influential worldwide.

In any case, when Malcolm died, the Muslims who belonged to the New York temple simultaneously broke away from the Nation of Islam headquarters in Chicago, which at that time was headed by Elijah Mohammed, the founder of the Muslim group in America. Then, 20 years after the death of Malcolm X, the Muslims broke up again and splintered into smaller groups. All told, there are about 10 million Muslims in the US today.[7] Most of them are Mideast nationals.

AMERICAN MILITARY POWER

Prior to World War II, the US had a small military. Besides the Americas, it hardly had any military presence elsewhere. After FDR entered WWII where the theaters of warfare were across the Atlantic and in the Pacific, the US built a huge army and converted most civilian use of steel and even sugar for military use. With the defeat of Germany

7 https://en.wikipedia.org/wiki/Islam_in_the_United_States

and Japan, the US became the sole superpower. But this did not last long because the Soviets and US allies caught up.

So began the Cold War, and after US Diplomat Kagan suggested containing the Soviets around the world, the US established military bases in England, Spain, Italy, Germany, Greece, Turkey, Asia, Japan, Philippines, Thailand, Liberia, Australia and Cuba. This policy of containing the Soviets or communists led the US into Korea where it fought a standstill battle with China. All told, the US today has about 500 military bases and it sells about $2 billion of arms to foreign countries worldwide each year.[8] The German and Japanese subsidize the presence of American troops on their soil. Now, it appears some Japanese are really resentful to pay for the presence of American troops on their soil because there are 32 military bases on the island of Okinawa alone. When US soldiers on the military bases commit some serious crimes such as rape, they are not tried in Japanese courts but are flown to the US to face light sentences. Also, American military jets in Okinawa create noise, pollution, runoff, and the American soldiers are rowdy.

Many Americans and foreign-born don't know the US spends close to $1 trillion per year to maintain its military bases, aircrafts, and troops on the ground. With a national debt of $30 trillion, there is fear such a massive expenditure in times of peace might not be sustainable in the long run. President Joe Biden and his party must think the debt will go away, for they keep piling on the debt.

In the meantime, there are some Americans who have left the US to work for higher wages at American military bases

---

8 https://247wallst.com › special-report › 2020/03/09
https://www.state.gov › u-s-arms-transfers-increased-by-2-...

overseas, including in Guam, the Philippines, and Germany. And on a typical base there are schools for the soldiers' children, good food, medical facilities, and other benefits they couldn't have gotten if they were living stateside. As an added bonus, their bathrooms are swept two to three times per day, and they shop tax-free at the commissary.[9] It seems everyone except me is enjoying that debt overload.

Blacks and other non-Whites constitute 40% of the US Army, and 50% of all US Army females are Black women. All the top US Marine generals are White men. Uncle Sam should be tactful, for an uncontrolled racial turmoil can spill over into the military and undermine morale.

Overall, the laws of the US, unlike other countries, have prevented the US military from interfering in its domestic policies. But the Insurrection Act enacted post-Civil War permits the President to call in the militia to put down disturbances in various states as it nearly happened on 1/6/2021.

VIETNAM TRAGEDY HITS CLOSE TO HOME

At its height, America had close to 500,000 troops on the ground in Vietnam. The US was led by General Westmoreland. Then Nixon and Henry Kissinger came along and sought rapprochement with China and the Soviet Union to relax world tension. In all those instances of threats and wars, none of the major powers used a nuclear weapon. This showed how much the world had matured.

Even though the War in Vietnam had been going on since 1965 or so, apart from news reports from Newsweek, the

---

9 Chalmers Johnson,'Nemesis: The Last Days of the American Republic', a Hold Paperback.

New York Times, and the BBC, it was hard to see someone who actually went to Vietnam, fought, and came back home safely.

I had this gap in my brain filled when a friend of mine, Geraldine, introduced me to her brother David Hinton sometime in 1973. At that time, the family lived in White Plains or Westchester, New York. From David I learned about the brutality of that war and how he was discharged dishonorably. This occurred when a group of Black soldiers in his platoon had refused to charge upon a hill. However, their White Commander should have known it was a fruitless task.

So, for insubordination, David Hinton and his group were dishonorably discharged, which meant none were entitled to any post-duty benefits. But this wasn't the end of Hinton's problems, for he soon found out from Uncle Sam that his common-law Vietnamese wife he had met in Vietnam couldn't be admitted to the US, since technically they were not married. Also, the American government would not allow Hinton to return to Vietnam because it had become a war zone where the government couldn't guarantee his and his fiancé's safety.

Mr. Hinton, amidst all this, became depressed, and he had no one to turn to. I recall his father once worked as part of the maintenance crew fixing the rail tracks of the New York subway system. But he became bedridden from asthma. He really suffered, and every 5 minutes he would wheeze out loud while in bed. At that time, I did not know Hinton could have written his Congressman for help.

The second time I saw a Black Vietnam Veteran was in 1973 when another friend from Harlem introduced her friend to me who had returned home briefly from Vietnam and was getting ready to return. I did not get to know this tall West Indian man much, but I soon heard that he had been killed in combat in Vietnam. No one could tell me what was his rank, in what province he died, or how long he was there. Minorities in general forget each other really quickly.

This, too, is among the tragedies that occur regularly in minority communities. Both large and small events are easily forgotten, for we don't write things down. I imagine if I had kept up with this soldier's letters and his experiences at the war front, today the Army could have erected a statue for him to make us all proud of his service. Or even if my friend Lillian McIllwan had stayed in touch with this guy, at least we could have gotten Kevin Shruggs, the Head of the Vietnam group, to have included this West Indian Veteran's profile on the Memorial Wall in Washington, DC. This would have brought some closure to his death.

Apart from major wars there have been some minor skirmishes involving Americans that the larger public is not readily aware of. An example was the Bay of Pigs that failed to oust Castro. Then there was the culmination of East/West conflict in a nuclear crisis over Cuba. And not long ago, US Navy Seals descended on some Iraqi natives celebrating a wedding in the middle of the night and ruined the whole party. And there have been other incidents like President Jimmy Carter's attempt to rescue about 44 American citizens from Iran in 1979. That ended in a fiasco. There was no Congressional hearing over the performance of US forces and the public never learned about the details. Well, those are some of the stories the Pentagon keeps away from the public. So, this is all part of the America we don't know.

PART III

Reflections and Perspectives on America

Chapter 7

America's Class System

In the political realm post-slavery, minorities have come a long way. We now have Black Mayors in D.C., Atlanta, Richmond, and other places. The Attorney General of New York is a Black female. All this came about from a political system that has two main parties, and both could be found at the local, state, and federal levels of government. It's real progress, with just about 50 years of LBJ's equal housing initiatives, equal opportunity in jobs, and Brown v. Topeka also opening the door to the educational advancement of Blacks.

BARRIERS IN EDUCATION

The problem with Black schools, beginning from elementary school all the way to the top, starts with the neglect of local jurisdictions to adequately fund them. Up to the high school level, some don't have good and contemporary books, and science lab tools and equipment are outdated. All of this affects the academic standing of students when they make their way through college. Eventually, Black students are not adequately prepared to compete in the job market, limiting their ability to earn a high income. It's estimated that 28% of all high school age minorities either never enroll or drop out of school.[10]

With so much progress having been made, especially in minority-run colleges like Morgan State, Howard, and Fisk Universities, foreign-born Blacks who grew up under the British system of education could find the American system much easier, because the British system appeared repressive and sought to preserve the class system in the colonies. With that said, the American system of education had its own class system, too. For example, most of the White students who went to Harvard Business School were no different academically from other average students, except they were White and came from wealthy families. In fact, their LSAT scores weren't as great, but upon graduation they easily found jobs.

Furthermore, large banks such as Chase Manhattan, Citibank, Chemical Bank, and Manufacturing Hanover Bank are all places I and other foreign-born students couldn't get into at one time or the other. LBJ tried to mitigate this barrier. A residual barrier still exists, as seen by the Asian students at Yale and Harvard recently launching a campaign for the courts to address this issue.

BARRIERS IN EMPLOYMENT AND EQUAL HOUSING

On the housing front, America's chief propaganda during the Cold War with the Soviet Union was having one nation indivisible by class or anything. But it doesn't take long to

10 Report of the National School Boards Association, "Black Students in the Condition of Education 2020", https://nsba.org/ Perspectives/2020/black-students-condition-education

find out that a White person could easily get an apartment or job faster than a Black person could in places like New York or Boston. See 'Deaths of Despair and the Future of Capitalism' where authors Case and Deaton explain that the structure in this county evolved from bondage and post bondage, i.e. Jim Crow[11]. In fact, less than a month ago, Joe Biden himself said on TV that there is no racism in America. However, everyone knows he did not mean it. As stated, employment and housing carry the scars of the past. And Harlem, New York and Roxbury in Boston, are the reflections of the scars.

HOW COME THERE ARE SO MANY HOMELESS IN THE RICHEST PART OF THE WORLD?

Through much of the 60s, there were few homeless people as I recall in New York. We used to call them winos on the stoops. But the homeless populations shot up 1,000% in the 1970s when some landlords began to intentionally burn down their buildings—especially in the Bronx—in order to collect on the insurance proceeds.[12] As a result, many people who used to reside in old tenements and projects got thrown to the streets. When ex-Mayor Koch of New York and David Dinkins said that the city did have the resources to house everyone, the government opened several shelters for the homeless and even went to the extent of renting hotels to house the homeless. What was supposed to be temporary housing became permanent over time. This also happened in D.C. when the old hospital at D.C. General

---

11 'Deaths of Despair and the Future of Capitalism' by Ann Case and Angus Deaton, Princeton University Press, 2020
12 https://ny.curbed.com/2019/5/3/18525908/south-bronx-fires-decade-of-fire-vivian-vazquez-documentary

became the home for some families for about 20 years. But some of these relocated individuals did prefer to live under bridges or to return to abandoned buildings in Baltimore, gas stations, and schools. But New York did not expend as much money on this population as San Francisco did when in 2019, it spent $852 million on the homeless.[13] But that hasn't reduced the homeless population.

To a foreigner not accustomed to such huge human cargoes, it becomes baffling as to who is in charge of homeless Americans sleeping in trains and under bridges. Occasionally, one may see a homeless African male sleeping in the woods, but African women never stay in shelters, for their extended family connections usually come to rescue them. Foreigners should be alerted to this tragic part of American life where no one cares about where you sleep at night. A homeless person may have a regular job, but it may not be enough to pay for rent. Simply put, since changes in wages haven't caught up with the cost of living, a household of four that makes less than $80,000 per year can't afford a one bedroom apartment in a place like San Francisco. New York may be slightly less, but the least slip in yearly income can cause that family to become homeless. It's high time Americans tackled this issue with a bold plan.

STATE SANCTIONED THEFT IN AMERICA

One other thing which non-White foreign-born may not know is that despite labor laws enacted by both state and federal arms of government, some crooked employers prefer immigrants and independent laborers or even skilled

---

13 https://www.hoover.org/research/only-san-francisco-61000-tents-and-350000-public-toilets

labor to 'work' for them and then stiff them on taxes and deny them benefits.

This is a recurring pattern that frequently happens to factory workers, nannies, garden boys, and migrant workers at job sites far from home. In fact, D.C. law firm Steptoe and Johnson informally settled a large sum of money due to some Hispanic immigrants from a big American contractor a few years ago. Obviously, the immigrant workers' language limitations played a part.

I did not know this deception until years later when the same issue hit us. This happened when Costco, the retail chain in Arlington, sought our services to scout land they could use for further expansion. My spouse and I surveyed about a dozen sites from Delaware to Baltimore. Twelve weeks later, after we prepared our report to Costco, Mr. Leuck refused to pay us $60,000. Their action amounts to the free labor the American Negro expended to build this country. In fact, no American news service will broadcast such an adverse outcome.

DELINQUENT POLITICIANS

American Congressman Steny Hoyer is an example of an ineffective politician. I recall for all the 38 years we spent living in Prince George's County in Maryland, Mr. Hoyer never came around until the last week before each national election. It would be better if he donated his salary to a homeless organization or to Father Flanagan's Boys Town.

Another unhelpful politician was Barbara Mikulski. For 20 years I sought her help to ward off the Small Business Administration and Judge Messitte of Maryland from stealing our warehouses. I wrote her several letters and visited her Baltimore office several times. However, my efforts were to no avail. In a debt collection case where the debt collector, Emil Hirsch, had no standing, he conspired with Judge Messitte and Prosecutor Rosenstein who issued an injunction and a restraining order. This application sent me to jail for a long time such that when I came back my business was ruined. Judge Messitte warned my lawyer, Paul Kramer, that he would jail him, too, if he continued defending me. I did not know then that the due process doesn't apply all the time in America.

Parren Mitchell, a humble Black Congressman from Baltimore always did work hard to assist small businesses both white and non-white.

Another politician who was unhelpful is Ms. Eleanor Holmes. For all the years we have lived in the D.C. area, Ms. Holmes has always dodged us when we show up at her offices looking for help to untangle a government regulation. But in her youthful days she did find time to jog beside Bill Clinton.

There are issues that come up now and then, and frustrated homeowners may end up joining an extreme group or listening to people at the fringe because the political leadership has failed them. These are the things that many Americans don't know about the system. They would rather swallow their losses because their political leadership has failed them.

However, my wife and I should give credit to some good politicians we have met, like the late Marion Barry, ex-Mayor of D.C. He helped us to get government contracts when we started our business. Another good politician was Parren Mitchell, a Baltimore Congressman. Also, US

Senator Ted Kennedy of Massachusetts did help, providing assistance for one of my sisters to come to the US with a green card. Kennedy also gave me my first government job. Former President George Bush, Sr., was also very helpful to my siblings. Now, even if a handful of today's politicians were as good as the old ones, there would be less frustration in American society.

Later we did find out that the best method to make a politician do you favors is to contribute to his political campaign. And if you need big help, you go out and hire a lobbyist. Some lobbyists are lawyers, and some others are former congressmen. Here since the Big Boys are at play, it gets expensive to employ them. But this informed group is a key part of the machinery of government.

Chapter 8:

Justice the American Way; Big Rip-Offs of Minorities in American Courtrooms

Contrary to what the average person has been led to believe, the American courtroom is not a neutral forum or a place where a minority's due process is respected. Some judges are un-American, and others collude with the opposing counsel. For example, Judge Peter J. Messitte uses the US Marshal Service and the FBI to shake down defendants. Neither the New York Times nor the Washington Post publishes these abuses. Another example is one Dr. Cooke of Montgomery County, Pennsylvania did a psychological profile of me back in 2008-2009 and charged me almost $2,000. But it was a hearsay report, because I never met or saw or spoke with psychologist Cooke. Rod J. Rosenstein, the then US Prosecutor, and my lawyer knew what was going on. And instead of asking presiding Judge J.R. Goodwin to exclude the report from the proceedings, they allowed the judge to include the phony psychiatric report in sentencing me, claiming I was mentally unwell. I was lucky, for the judge could have sent me to a mental hospital forever. Usually a prosecutor's role remains hidden, but they can shape the outcome of a case.

Many Americans may not know that the jurisdiction of John Roberts, the Supreme Court Chief Justice is limited to the Supreme Court building only. From the look of things, Roberts has no authority over Appeals and District Court judges. Thus, Roberts is the head of another branch of government that appears to be toothless. But how does he collect a salary as much as the Vice President of the United States plus free coffee and newspapers every morning? To save taxpayers from this rut, perhaps the Chief Justice should be confined to 20-year term limits and District Court Judges to 10 years to save them from boredom.

But despite being seemingly isolated from the average person, there have been Supreme Court Justices like Thurgood Marshall and Earl Warren who cared for the Little Guy.

Admittedly, there are lots of things about the law that we don't know. This perhaps leads to a high incarceration of minorities, including the foreign born. For example, if the police removes an item from a defendant's personal property unlawfully, the police, according to the law, cannot use the seized item to prosecute and convict the defendant, for that will amount to a violation of the defendant's Fourth Amendment rights. The defendant can seek a retrial.[14] But many minority defendants don't know about this right and can easily get convicted if their Public Defender attorneys look the other way.

---

14 Riley v. California, 573 U.S. 373

Another law that is usually violated by law enforcement is that a police officer should have probable cause to seek an arrest or to search without warrant under emergency. This is also known as 'exigent circumstances'. But a police officer should have probable cause even without a warrant before he can search or arrest a suspect. A non-exigent warrant should be notarized and should be free from hearsay or else it becomes inadmissible. These are all issues that many minorities don't know.

My impression is that many American judges are not too bright, like Judge Reggie Walton of the US District Court in Washington or Judge Alexander Williams of the US District Court in Maryland. I remember about 25 years ago the US Senate withheld his nomination because it had concerns about Williams' writing ability. Williams is a Howard University Alumnus. My spouse and I rallied alongside others for Williams, and he got nominated. Similarly, in a public forum in 2009, US District Court Judge Walton admitted that until he was 17 he was semi-illiterate and couldn't read and write. Note that both Williams and Walton are black. I immediately understood what he was talking about and why he hated me when ex-Federal Prosecutor Rosenstein and his friends threw me into jail after their friends stole our assets. And that is why I planned to use that knowledge to write this book that will educate people about the pitfalls people don't know in the American courtroom.

To curb abuses, federal judgeships should be limited to 10 years, Supreme Court Justices should be limited to 20 years, and criminal records should be erased after a defendant has fully served his time, probation, and has fully paid his court fine. So there won't be any request for a pardon or continuing harassment of ex-offenders.

Now, if American civilization is to be led by people like Judges P.J. Messitte, Alexander Williams, and Prosecutor Rosenstein this nation has no future. To illustrate, in a case we had before him he thought that because we are Black we wouldn't know what to do. I recall on the first day of pretrial hearings before we had a chance to hire lawyers, Messitte told the US Marshal on duty that after he photographed and fingerprinted me and my spouse, we should be detained until Messitte had a chance to decide if we were going home that night or not. But the strange thing was that the case was being handled by Judge Derby in the Bankruptcy Court. And Judge Messitte usually handled non-bankruptcy matters. Somehow, he had reached into the Bankruptcy Court and took away to his courtroom the matter under deliberation. He gave away $2 million of our assets to his foot soldier and friend Emil Hirsch, the debt collector. Judge Messitte is White and a graduate of Northwestern Law School. And when I fought back, Messitte had me thrown into jail for a long time such that when I came back from jail our business was ruined.

Lawyers we hired like Paul Kramer, Stanley Alpert and Maher captained by Michael Schatzow, a former US Prosecutor, and F.W. Bennett and 15 others all turned out to be turncoats secretly working to turn over our assets to creditor Emil Hirsch and Judge Messitte. Unbelievably, Judge Messitte threatened all our lawyers with criminal contempt if they were to defend us or block his way to seize our assets. See US case #PJM03-2241. All told, we spent $1 million in legal fees because the lawyers would quit under Messitte's threats, and we would have to get another set of lawyers who would charge more. This is how Messitte slowly bleeds people to death. And people who don't know the details of this case still ask why we don't get lawyers. Amidst all this, no one lifted a finger to help us. This taught me that my white male friends don't take any prisoners and they shied away from us. Further, pleading to President Obama and his wife and Joe Biden went nowhere. I did not know how the American system worked.

Months later, Messitte stepped off the bench and came down to testify against me. This is the same judge who had earlier tried me in a criminal contempt case in May 2004. Obviously, this was a conflict. But Obama did nothing, and later on we learned that Rod J. Rosenstein, the Maryland US Prosecutor, was Obama's Harvard schoolmate and Obama didn't want to shame Rosenstein or any of his Harvard or Chicago friends by helping us. This is a violation of my Due Process I did not know when I left Ghana to the US.

INTRODUCTION TO AMERICAN LAW

First, the backbone of American jurisprudence is made up of the police on the street, private lawyers, government lawyers, and prosecutors. We then climb to the courthouse where we meet various judges, and if we go further federal prosecutors and the Supreme Court. No one knows that about 300 years ago when we partially adopted British Law where King William I gathered with his court and his lords and ladies to accept the reduction of the powers of the King, this meant the King couldn't come to your backyard to steal your food or wife without probable cause. And if a citizen is prosecuted, he will be entitled to the Due Process at the legal front. But the right to a hearing and the Due Process that protects you and I are quickly being eroded.

Chapter 9

American Police and Criminal Justice

More than 100 years ago, there were hardly any policemen in America. It was the rich people who had factories in Michigan and Massachusetts and their own police force to watch over the unions and their factories. It was men like Henry Ford who could afford them. But with the increase of the population in places like New York, Chicago, and Los Angeles, and their growing suburbs full, professional forces have been hired by local, state, and federal authorities. Partly prior to the Patriot Act, the 1994 legislation enacted by the Clinton Administration, Clinton gave state governments enough money to hire an extra 100,000 policemen in various communities. He also tightened sentencing, including the '3 Strikes, and You Are Out' rule. Unfortunately, this evolved into mass incarceration of Black men. No one spoke against this until Bill Clinton himself apologized for this heavy handedness during the 2016 campaign.

All told, the nation today has about a million policemen of various names and descriptions. One in eight is a female and one in four is a minority. Here are some of the US policing groups, namely:

- FBI
- Drug Enforcement Agency
- Department of Homeland Security
- US Treasury Agents
- State, City, and County Police
- Campus Police at colleges
- Housing Inspectors
- Towns and Village Constables
- And many more we don't even know about
- The Secret Service

Current Head Count of Police Officers in the US

Type of Agency	# of Full-time Sworn Officers	Percentage of the Total
Local Police	461,063	52%
State Police	60,772	23%
Special Police	55,968	6%
Federal Police	120,348	14%
Estimated total = about 1 million officers		

Sources:
Brian A. Reaves, Federal Law Enforcement Offices 2000, Washington, D.C. Census of State and Local Law Enforcement Agencies, 2008 Washington, D.C. INS Bureau of Justice Statistics, 2011

Usually in America the police you see walking on the street are engaged in community policing with the intent of keeping order. Some enforce traffic rules, help out with fire service, rescue stray dogs, and give rides to pregnant women late for delivery. They also fight crimes, and it has been widely reported many of those policemen on the beat occasionally get into fights with some people who happen to be Black. But many people don't know that the vast majority of people arrested are White. But these culprits are hardly killed by White policemen. Part of the reason for White police tension with Black men is that most of these policemen hail from rural Pennsylvania and upstate New York or areas where Whites don't have much interaction with Blacks when they are growing up. So, these White policemen are more likely to use force or their guns to solve problems because they don't know or understand non-Whites and in some cases are not well-educated.

Many people don't know that a policeman can shoot a pedestrian or kill someone sitting at his home and get away with it. Even many don't know in an emergency the police can search your person or your home without a warrant. See New York Times of 9/25/2020, the case of Breonna Taylor, the tragedy of a woman from Kentucky. See New York Times of 9/24/2020, front page. Also, see American System of Criminal Justice by George C. Cole et al, 'Policing Contemporary Issues and Challenges', Chapter 7, p. 329.

AMERICAN LAWYERS AND JUDGES: WHO POLICES THEM?

Lawyers are components of the American justice system and law enforcement, but most lawyers are unethical. If you were to go to court to recover funds and the judge finds out that you are suing a lawyer, by all means the judge will take the side of the lawyer defendant. The reason for this is the judge used to steal from clients when he was a lawyer, before he became a judge. Thus, to go after his fraternal brother you are just reminding him of all the petty crimes he himself committed before he rose up. Lawyers' fraternity stretches from the traffic court to everywhere. For example, there are many public issues Mr. and Mrs. Clinton, Obama and his wife, Joe Biden and VP Harris will not get into just because they are lawyers, and the other side are lawyers, too. This is how public morale has fallen.

Some judges get gifts like expensive wine and jewelry from lawyers who appear before them, including Judge E. Stephen Derby of the Bankruptcy Court in Baltimore. He puts on jewelry and wears $1,000 suits, but where does he get this money from? On the government's paycheck? And there was Judge Herman Dawson of the PG Circuit Court system in Upper Marlboro, Maryland. He was openly a thief without being shy about it. The FBI knew this but did nothing because he was a stooge for them. He colluded with Joseph Buonassissi, a lawyer from Northern Virginia who represented mortgage companies, almost all in Prince George's County, Maryland, for PG County is lax in enforcing the law.

In Prince George's County, Buonassissi will file false claims against homeowners. Usually, the homeowner won't be able to fight back because under Maryland law to fight a mortgage foreclosure you have to post a bond. And if the balance on one's mortgage is $100,000 then the homeowner has to come up with $200,000 to buy the bond to stay the foreclosure proceeding. But none of the people I know in PG County have that kind of money. So back in the year 2008 and 2010 when there was a mortgage crisis, Joseph Buonassissi became wealthy and worked in tandem with Judge Herman Dawson. Allegedly, Dawson had a foundation for the benefit of Black children, but nobody has ever seen these Black children, and the only benefactors of Dawson's foundation were the lawyers who appeared before him. This apparently is a conflict of interest. So, I wrote Governor O'Malley, an Irish bully from Baltimore who was a lawyer by profession. But O'Malley ignored me. The FBI knew about Dawson being a crook, too, but also did nothing. This is because if Agent Simmons needs an inadmissible warrant to arrest signed, he could get Dawson to do his dirty work for him.

Having spent over '35 years' to '40 years in the D.C./ Maryland area, I have encountered so many corrupt lawyers. Key among them is old worn-out Paul Kramer who technically has retired from appearing in the courtroom, but is so adept in trading his Black clients, shepherding them to pleas they don't deserve and reaping profits from them. I did not know all this can occur in the 'Land of the Free'.

I didn't know Americans were afraid of their judges until I came here. It's logical, too, to assume that judges are chosen from a pool of lawyers and most lawyers are unethical and money hungry.

In the year 2000, my wife and I were summoned to court because Emil Hirsch, the same a debt collector for New York mortgage company Pramco mentioned earlier, had filed a complaint pursuant to a demand note that we owed some money. When we appeared before Judge Peter J. Messitte of Greenbelt, Maryland one morning, his first order of business was to order the US Marshal on duty to stand above our shoulders like we were about to run away. Then a couple of minutes later Messitte told the Marshal to accompany us to the basement so that the Marshal will take our pictures and fingerprints. I told the judge that since this is the first hearing, we need to hire a lawyer and let him represent us, and that he is criminalizing a simple debt collection. Until this incident I never knew people went to prison for debt in America, especially if the debtor has no standing. Anyway, he retorted that after the fingerprinting was done, we should go and wait at the US Marshals Office so that he will deliberate whether he will allow us to go home or not that evening. At this point, all my reading of American 'Rule of Law' and the 'Right to a Hearing' were thrown out of the window.

Fortunately, the US Marshal on duty late that afternoon told Judge Messitte that what he was doing should come at the end of a hearing, but he couldn't summarily throw us into jail, for the Marshal could not carry out such an order.

The whole point is that Messitte thought that because we are Black, we are stupid, and that a minority could have a million dollars and still be considered stupid. That is what it is. Eventually Messitte, using injunctions and restraining orders, did tie up our hands and summarily stole about $2,000,000 of our assets. But he couldn't have done it without a big help from his friend US Prosecutor R.J. Rosenstein, the then United States Attorney for Maryland and his sidekick, Alexander Williams, a Black judge, and the FBI.

Up to now, there is no proof in the court records that Pramco's debt collector, Emil Hirsch, had standing to have collected even a dime from us to result in liquidation of our estate. Lawyers we hired like Michael Schatzow, a former US Attorney in Maryland, Paul Kramer, and about 18 others refused to help us get our assets back or to stop Messitte from enforcing his phony restraining orders. Generally, they were afraid that Messitte was going to find them in criminal contempt for helping us. Here one clearly sees how a judge, lawyers, prosecutors, and debt collectors combine to wreak havoc on the Little Guy.

Outside the courtroom we found that White people we thought were our friends and had nothing to do with the case did turn their backs on us, and this encouraged Messitte to rob us. Among them was Dr. Jack Luther, a retired Economist at Dept. of Labor; Donald Graham, the former publisher of the Washington Post and my pen pal then; and Dr. Donald Brenner, a lawyer and a professor at American University. Al Gordon, a D.C. Attorney and other White men who were not connected to our case somehow found a way to avoid us. I still believe that because Judge Messitte and his henchman, Emil Hirsch, are White, and I and my spouse are Black and I am foreign-born, it was all right for them to help Messitte with their silence. I have now concluded that a federal judge in his black robe and sitting on the bench is so powerful that the President of the United States won't even go near him.

DOES THE FBI SAFEGUARD CITIZENS' DUE PROCESS?

All told, there are about a million law enforcement officers in the US today. At the national level, the FBI is very prominent with a staff of about 13,913 and 22,000 support professionals that include scientists, language translators, computer experts, and intelligence analysts. Its main functions include fighting white-collar crime to protect the US from nefarious foreign intelligence agencies. Elsewhere at the Department of Justice are several agencies, including the Drug Enforcement Agency and the US Marshal Service.

In addition, the US Department of Health and Human Services investigates Medicaid fraud.

When it comes to federal crime, one may more likely encounter the FBI instead of local Baltimore police. But one should not be fooled by the FBI's neat appearance of a white shirt, tie, and jacket. This is because a typical FBI Agent is a zombie wound up for misconduct by a judge like Messitte whose inclination is to misuse the FBI for his end. The FBI generally are considered 'Yes Men' and they don't ask many questions of their bosses. I understand most of them come from Utah, and others like New York firefighters are of Irish descent.

Well it did not take too long to encounter the FBI, for one morning while this Messitte thing was going on, one FBI Agent named Thomas Simmons knocked at our door in Beltsville, Maryland, and he asked to speak to me. So, when I said, "Yes," he put me in handcuffs right away. He never asked our permission to enter the door nor did he utter any probable cause. And he said he had reports I was going 'to shoot a judge'. I told him it was not true, but he said he had to take me to his office and take me to court for a hearing.

I wasn't read my Miranda rights when FBI Agent Thomas Simmons arrested me on May 2, 2005. See Miranda v Arizona, 1966. At least I was in police custody and Simmons ought to have read me my rights and cite a probable cause. Now, if he had read me my Miranda rights, he should have told me that I could remain silent if I wanted to; if I were to make any statement, that statement could be used against me; that I had the right to have an attorney present during interrogation or the right to consult an attorney or the state could provide one if I couldn't afford one. See Dickerson

v. U.S. (2000). Also, see Pennsylvania v. Muniz, 1990. An 'exogenous' circumstance may require a law enforcement or police officer to make a warrantless search without probable cause. But the Affidavit in support of a warrant shouldn't contain hearsay.

Virtually, the FBI is a state within a state, and I was beginning to understand what was happening. Someone once told me that the modus operandi of the FBI was that if a neighbor or a friend were to go to them and alert them that a subject is engaged in a criminal activity, somehow the FBI wouldn't go after the subject who is allegedly breaking the law, but rather go after the good guy(s) who brought them that information. I had earlier written Director Mueller about the alleged corruption of Judges Derby, Messitte and Prosecutor Rosenstein. And instead of the FBI doing its job to investigate the named culprits, they found it much easier to throw me in jail to keep my mouth shut. To me, the FBI is a cabal given their history of nefarious activities from the Nixon era to today. See the Mueller Report-2019.[15]

Ironically, when I first arrived in New York in the early 70s there was a fictional show about the FBI that came on weekly. Efrem Zimbalist, Jr. and his buddy were my favorite actors, and they always got their man. I did not know one day they would arrest me with a fake warrant to get their man.

Apart from its original function of catching car thieves and bank robbers, as dictated by Hoover, the FBI has expanded globally with missions in foreign lands. It also runs a counter spying operation in the United States even to the extent to snooping on US citizens.

---

15 Robert S. Mueller, III, 'The Mueller Report', Melville House Publishing, April 2019.

Recently a federal court in Washington ruled that government broad surveillance of American citizens for their personal data is wrong. In fact, the FBI has increased its might not only beyond collection of data, but also its surveillance of US citizens whether or not they posed any threat. In sum, the FBI is a State within a State subsidized and paid for by the frightened American taxpayer.

SOME OF THE GOOD THINGS THE POLICE DO

Many years ago a friend of mine's wife, Ama, on her return home after work somehow got lost. After her husband and friends roamed through the streets and trains in the Bronx, the police were able to locate her at midnight in no time at all and return her to her husband. Ama was so scared by this incident that she quit her night shift job and sought to divorce her husband Ken Addo. Now, if Ama had sought help from the police right away riding the subway that night, she would not have roamed through the streets. Unfortunately, Ama was a new immigrant and was afraid the police would turn her over to the immigration authorities. There are numerous reports about the Police rescuing people by helping to deliver babies on the road to rescuing accident victims from car wrecks.

On the other hand, it appears the police are in some type of undeclared war against Black American males. Part of it is that most American police in New York City or Boston originally were raised in rural Pennsylvania or upstate New York. And these people grew up without much interaction with Blacks. One suggestion is for each police jurisdiction to have its own ombudsman to resolve matters quickly outside the courtroom.

David Kissi

THE PITFALL THAT CAN BEFALL FOREIGNERS ON AMERICAN SOIL

Despite the propaganda that America is next to Heaven, no one ever advised me in advance that a foreigner can come here and despite all his accomplishments the System won't have respect for him deep down. I cite my case where Federal Judge Peter J. Messitte of Greenbelt, Maryland, who in May 2004 tried me in a criminal contempt case and the same judge in August 2006 did get off the bench and testified against me in a criminal trial in Baltimore. When I brought this conflict to the attention of the Chief Federal Judge in Maryland and the Court of Appeals for the 4th Circuit in Richmond and Rod Rosenstein, the then US Prosecutor for Maryland, and John Roberts, head of the Supreme Court, all ignored me.

I didn't know a foreigner's assets could be summarily seized and handed over to a White man even though such a White man may also be a foreigner himself and have no proof of ownership. A judge like Peter J. Messitte can tell my lawyers representing me in his court that they should desist from doing so or else he will find them in contempt. And when you get here the Black Congressional Caucus, and the NAACP will turn their backs on you. All this is the America I did not know.

I have also found out that no one can protect you once the judges and prosecutors turn against you until all your assets are stolen by the other side. For example, in this case with Emil Hirsch and Pramco, the presiding Judge J.R. Goodwin brought with him from West Virginia a young lady who looked and acted as his girlfriend but was the court's stenographer.

I did not think about it until after I ordered all the trial transcripts, and this same stenographer was paid $8,000 for labor. It was then I realized she had largely fabricated the transcript. For example, I had responded 'no' to a question in the court, but she made it 'yes' and it was vice versa throughout. When I brought this to Goodwin's attention, Messitte managed to have me banned from all federal courthouses in Maryland, and that is where matters have stood for 20 years. The stenographer's fraud rendered the criminal conviction against me as hearsay, and the entire case should have been dismissed. But Goodwin denied that motion. See U.S. 05-cr-0254.

Despite the other side's antics, I ended up in jail for obstruction of justice. And after my imprisonment, D.C. Superior Court Judge Macaluso informed me that it was more likely I would get our assets back in her courtroom. But this never happened because after the next appearance she disappeared from the courthouse. Then her Associate Judge Michael Rankin who took over those cases told me that if I didn't drop the cases against Pramco, he was going to cite me for criminal contempt and put me in jail. Then Rankin, a Black judge, relayed this incident to his fellow Federal Judge Alexander Williams of the Greenbelt, Maryland courthouse where Judge Messitte was. Alexander Williams, without a fair hearing or looking at the facts, had me locked up for a probation violation in 2013. So, in other words, my case that occurred in Maryland moved to D.C. and D.C. sent the case back to Maryland that has been hostile to me. So, if this is not corruption to keep us from our assets, then what is it?

Now, everyone who has heard this tragic story wonders where were our lawyers? Well my wife and I had over 20 lawyers over a 20-year period and virtually all of them were turncoats. Now, the most dangerous lawyers I encountered were former government lawyers who were mainly delivering me to their friend, R.J. Rosenstein who was on Emil Hirsch's and Mortgage Banker Pramco's payroll. But why should I have to take a plea when Pramco's debt collector Emil Hirsch had no standing and had committed perjury that could be used to have my conviction overturned on appeal? But none of this mattered to the trial court.

Another key reason why judges and lawyers are corrupt is that newspapers like the Washington Post and the New York Times would not publish their misdeeds. So, the bad guys get stronger and stronger. Judges are also powerful in American Courts. For example, one judge may set a bail bond for $20,000 and for the same crimes another judge will set the bond at $10,000. The same is applicable in sentencing where one judge is more severe than the other. This exercise of control is sometimes the cause of corruption. But someone like Mr. Trump, who makes people believe he fights for the Little Guy, would not dare to step on the toe of a judge because tomorrow he will need a judge's favor in a business deal or to restrain a strike against his business by a union.

The US Supreme Court is an island sealed off, and it doesn't want to hear how Messitte and Rosenstein continue to rip-off American Citizens. Even the fact that John D. Roberts, Rod Rosenstein, and Peter J. Messitte live in Bethesda, a Maryland suburb, requires us to show discretion and not speak too loudly about them. One should speak carefully because one doesn't know what these judges like Messitte and Kavanaugh discuss at their country club in Bethesda. This is the America a naïve foreigner does not know. Taxpayers pay over $200,000 per year to each of the 9 justices of the High Court with benefits of free coffee and

New York Times thrown in. But this is not enough, for we are supposed to be afraid of our judges.

The only justice I would favorably speak of is Justice William O. Douglas with whom I briefly corresponded with in the mid-70s before he died. At least he was an impartial justice. Earl Warren and Thurgood Marshall too were considered friends of the Little Guy when they sat on the High Court over 50 years ago.

The American public should be enlightened that the justices on the Supreme Court are humans like anybody else and once the public sees they could be unfair, perhaps the public could start to scrutinize their rulings. An example of the people's unhappiness with some of the High Court rulings was President Joe Biden's April 2021 proposal to assemble a panel of 35 public figures and academics (excluding me) to come up with suggestions to improve the courts.

This is an excellent idea because it could lead to shortening or limiting the High Court judge's tenure to 20 years. Perhaps it will also reduce boredom, for all of them appear bored when their yearly pictures are taken.

Even in the absence of people's complaints there has to be a periodic review of the functions of the courts in respect to whether we need them or not. Or alternative forums should be created to handle certain crimes. The reason behind this is when the American Constitution was first written the founding fathers didn't know anything about computers, telegraphs, or gay people. So, what this means is that the Supreme Court is trying to fit round pegs into square holes in matters that don't belong to the court.

Chapter 10

Minority Groups in America

US UNILATERAL SUPPORT FOR ISRAEL

When Israel declared its independence from the British Palestine Protectorate in 1948, Harry S. Truman, the then US President was among the first Heads of State to recognize the Jewish state. Thereafter, many American Jews did pour money into Israel to turn what was once a desert into a rich farmland of milk and honey.

At that time in 1967 we did not understand the full import of the underlying issues of the struggle over land and for shortages the Arabs imposed on the international oil market. Despite the damage to the American economy, the US kept its support for Israel 100%. The Arab position that the Israelis should return Jerusalem to Arab or Jordanian control did not go anywhere because the US used its veto power at the Security Council in New York to block any such transfers.

In 1968 there was a third Jewish/Arab conflict in which the United Nations intervened and stipulated that all future land agreements should be subject to negotiations supervised by the UN under Resolution 242 appended to the terms of the cease-fire agreement governing the Israeli/ Palestinian War of 1967. Now, this is where modern-day US has gone wrong. The United States, since the inception of Israel, has supported Israel and has literally given them modern arms at no cost subsidized by US taxpayers. And there are even reports of a secret US military base in Israel.

Then the Arabs did return in 1973 for the third time. This time their brave leader Anwar Sadat successfully breached Israel. But the UN Security Council called for both parties to resolve their conflict per peaceful resolution. The fate of Jerusalem was to be determined as part of a final settlement.

But the Israelis partly ignored that resolution and immediately went to work by settling Israelis on the West Bank.[16]

So, it wasn't a fluke after all when things boiled over in May 2021 when some Israelis started a fight near a Jewish/ Arab temple in Jerusalem. This violence went out of hand immediately. Jewish forces started carpet bombing and leveled Gaza, a tiny enclave with a population of about 2 million Palestinians. About 400 Arab Palestinians died. Joe Biden, who during the Presidential campaign had pledged to move away from the status quo just stood by even though he could have ordered the Israelis to stop the fighting since it was American arms and aircrafts being used to commit war crimes. But Israel did ignore Biden initially. [17]

---

16 See Wall Street Journal, 5/19/2021
17 See New York Times, 5/17/2021, front page.

US President Joe Biden who during the Presidential Campaign had pledged to move away from the status quo just stood by even though he could have ordered the Israelis to stop hostilities immediately or the Israelis should return the arms and aircrafts the Israelis had received without paying for them. For the Palestinians have no aircraft to counter the Israeli destruction. Certainly, the US unilateral support of Israel carries political cost at the United Nations.[18]

IS THE JEW OVERSOLD?

The State of Israel was founded mainly by Jewish immigrants from Russia after WWII. But prior to that there has been some limited flow of immigrants from Europe to Palestine. Be mindful the Romans had destroyed the temple in Jerusalem some centuries ago.

Many Americans don't know that before the British Palestine rule, some influential Jewish groups had contemplated establishing modern Israel in Uganda in Africa, but the proposal didn't fly. David Ben-Gurion was the first Israeli Prime Minister. Most of the early settlers settled in kibbutz and were farmers. In 1948 Israel declared itself independent of British rule. But this did provoke the Palestinians to attack them and Israel prevailed and increased their land size.

To some extent, the Israelis have much more sympathy in the United States than most other countries.[19] One reason is that there is a large Jewish population in New York who have been there forever running small businesses like law firms and clothing shops in the Garment District and Broadway theaters. And some are college professors

18 See The Wall Street Journal, Editorial 5/17/2021.
19 See The Washington Post, The Wall Street Journal and The New York Times, 5/19/2021, front pages.

who are in a position to influence students at young ages. So many people's first impression of the Jew is favorable. Two of the holiest days in Judaism are Passover and Yom Kippur. These are the best days when you can get a favor from a Jew.

Until now I did not know that the Jewish people one meets on college campuses are liberal, tolerant, and friendly to minorities, for the Jew considers themselves a minority group, too. But unfortunately, this perception doesn't really hold outside of college campuses where you meet debt collectors like Emil Hirsch who works as a foot soldier for cruel US judges like Peter J. Messitte of Maryland who unmercifully take the assets mostly of other minorities and summarily charge them for violating injunctions and restraining orders that have never been served. And generally, Jewish lawyers like Paul Kramer, Stanley Alpert, Granger Maher, Paul Epstein, Former US Prosecutor R.J. Rosenstein, Michael Schatzow, Walter Weir, and the late Fred W. Bennett et al usually turn out to be turncoats. It seems they have no loyalty to their clients except to their fellow Jews. But many Americans don't know this, and Jews as usual are more inclined to counter such statements as anti-Semitic. It seems their chief weapon in getting their way in the US is their whining and complaining.

Usually, Jewish newspapers like the New York Times and the Washington Post would not publish unflattering reports of Jewish individuals like Prosecutor Rod J. Rosenstein and my attorneys Paul Kramer and F.W. Bennett, et al. This is how the American press and unmerciful judges and lawyers keep the system going. Even Americans don't know their presidents and congressmen are afraid of the Jewish lobby.

But American Jews' tricks shouldn't blemish Jewish culture and history stretching back over 5,000 years from Abraham to King Solomon to Christ. And in our contemporary times we have had great Jewish historical figures like Sigmund Freud, Moshe Dayan, Arthur Goldberg, Golda Meir, Henry Kissinger, Barbara Streisand, and Woody Allen – all have been influential leaders.

In fact, all the above are my favorite Jews despite all the bad things Jews like Rosenstein and debt collector Emil Hirsch have done to us because we are not Jewish.   N o w , the conclusion to all the debate over the Middle East is the Jewish State should permit the return of the Palestinians who fled their homeland in 1948. A neutral America will serve as an arbiter to steer the Palestinians and Jews to a final consensus where the Jews will claim that area as a Jewish State and the other portion as a Palestinian State. But all this cannot be done while America is both a supporter and a bias arbiter in the conflict.[20]

Most Americans, even the well-educated ones, don't know some of the land the Jewish State claims as its own was once stolen from the Palestinians.

JEWISH HOUSEHOLDS

Jewish parents prefer first-born to be males like Abraham and Sarah bearing Jacob. Then the kid goes through circumcision and bar mitzvah. An uncircumcised Jew is classified as 'unwashed' until he is circumcised. There were periods in Europe when parents did not circumcise their kids in order to avoid or hide their Jewish heritage from authorities. The Jewish Yeshiva may be equivalent to our

---

20 See the Financial Times of London Editorial of 5/18/2021

American college and apart from studying the Torah, no one knows what else happens in there.

My favorite Jew is Marie Ann Altmann. This Jewish woman, for about 50 years, stood her ground to recover stolen works of art that the Nazis stole from her grandfather's collection in Vienna. After World War II, Ms. Altmann settled in New York and hired a lawyer to help her retrieve the artwork. Eventually, around 2005, she succeeded. She sold half of the art collection to Esther Lauder's son, and she gave away the other half to museums in the United States.

Ms. Altmann's resilience is remarkable for she had proved lots of people wrong. Similarly, the case of Herzog, the Jewish Art Collector drags on. The Herzog Collection of Art is still under litigation. And although the family got the assistance of Senator Ted Kennedy and Ms. Hillary Clinton, they have not made much headway, for the Government of Hungary claims ownership of the art collection. This provenance is further affirmed by Hungary since it paid for the collection and is now owner of the property.

The Herzog case has dragged on for more than 70 years without a settlement in sight.[21] I take consolation from Ms. Altmann and Herzog that one day we may achieve the impossible to get back our assets Emil Hirsch, Judge E. Stephen Derby and Judge Peter J. Messitte stole from us.

HOW THE WHITE MAN LOOKS AT NON-BLACKS

Non-white foreigners who are of no use to the White man are accorded little respect, for the White man by nature

---

21 See NY Times, 10/17/2020, p.5.

prefers not to take prisoners. Therefore, they are more likely to hire and live with non-Whites who can service their cars and trucks for them and engage in grounds keeping and assist their wives in their household duties.

I did find out that the Anglo-Saxon in North America prefers to live side-by-side with their own kind, and most of them are non-Catholic. A non-White will find it difficult to befriend them, especially if you didn't go to the same school with them or work with them.

Despite the stiffness of the White male in race relations, relatively speaking White women (especially those who are middle-aged or older) are more cordial, perhaps because of their nature to chat or they are curious of non-Whites in a harmless way. One is more likely to get neighborly important information from them. Sometimes, too, they feel their men have suppressed them and they need allies, so they are more inclined to help non-Whites. I did not know that about 100 years ago, suffragist Susan B. Anthony preached that if women were given the vote, they would become a significant political force. Well, it took only about 60 years to have the elderly women in Russia prove Ms. Anthony right, too. This is because when Russian President Boris Yeltsin's troops started harassing some demonstrators in the early 1990s, the troops quietly left the old women alone.

So, I researched this phenomenon and I saw the same in modern America where some women, meaning middle-aged and above, had gone to a great extent to help us. Mostly, all were White, some were business owners or worked for someone. But advancing age made them fearless. Some of these women were Harriet Bell, Mary Vincent,

Anna Hackman, Ms. Doss, Sherry Koonz, Ms. Myers, Sadie Montgomery (our Hyattsville, Maryland neighbor), Banker Ms. Piccolo, and others.

These are the things and individuals I did not know before coming to America. And they have proved helpful once I did find out about them.

Arabs and Persians make good and reliable friends, too, for they will never let you down. I had seen Arabs in Africa from a distance before I came to the US and years later when we organized a paper supply business. This was by chance since some of our customers were Arabs and others were Iranians. I noticed in my dealings with them that these people made very good friends and they were less likely to dump you, unlike White males, if one were to fall into trouble. When I visited their homes, they usually offered me a glass of water, and they were polite. At home the women wore western dresses.

Then there is the American Indian everyone has forgotten about until actor Marlon Brando resurrected them at the Oscars.

Speaking as a non-white foreign-born, I would say, Americans generally are superficially fair until you run into problems with them. To some Americans, foreigners who speak English with African, Asian, or Spanish accents are branded as semi-illiterates or dumb. Only Whites from Europe are exempt from this stereotype. But why Germans and Russians are excluded from the dummy group is a puzzle, for those two groups speak with some foreign accents, too.

In my case, despite the fact that I have taken speech lessons, I still have an accent, but a large part of our customer base is not bothered by my accent. If they were, none would have trusted me with their credit card information. I am not illiterate, for I do have several college degrees, which is more than the average American, and I speak other international languages, which many Americans don't.

Contemporary Americans should be proud and celebrate foreigners, for they are the ones who built modern America. Men like Henry Kissinger made this country famous. Yet Kissinger still speaks with a heavy German accent.

Talking to individuals or groups of people about characteristics they share or have in common shouldn't be construed as a stereotype. For example, an area of commonality shared by Hispanics and Africans is their disrespect of time. They usually forget or run late for appointments and deadlines. Also, neither of these groups write things down. So, they tend to forget the importance of dates and time, like when to see the dentist or attend their children's PTA meetings. One simple answer is to suggest to them to write things down to better assimilate into American society. What I am saying here are not stereotypes to degrade people. I am rather sharing my experiences with them as a fellow foreigner.

Lastly, I did also find that Hispanic people don't make easy friendships. Now, given their entrenched history of crossing the Rio Grande to get to the US and their harassment by the US Immigration, they tend not to put their roots in one place for a long time and are suspicious of strangers. Thus, the Spanish, like the Blacks suffer from a state of 'rootlessness' and as a result they find it difficult to get bank loans to start their own businesses. Usually, financial institutions will find them unstable.

Also, I didn't know anything about Asian people until I arrived in the US. But I did learn quickly that the Chinese are the dominant group among the Asians. And in Asia, China is branded as the Middle Kingdom. The Japanese are not too far behind. And their common meal is rice. Asians like Filipinos, Cambodians, Chinese, Vietnamese, and Koreans stick together. Generally, an outsider doesn't know what goes on in their opium den and car garages. Asians hardly interact with other non-Whites. But they do get along with Whites. They are mainly insular and prefer to stay in their little communities. They prefer to hire and work with individuals who look like them.

Furthermore, until I came to the US, I didn't know that the Black American didn't have too much in common with the African now coming from the African continent. Perhaps after 500 years of separation, the Black American is now much closer to the White man or European. The food they eat is more European, like hot dogs, frozen food, bacon, bread, and ice cream. These items are not staple foods in Africa. And obviously since they have been here so long the White and the African have apparently intermarried and the Black American today is not the same as the Blacks who first came to Jamestown, Virginia in 1619.

Overall, Blacks have done relatively well as mentioned in this memoir, and if the Black American group was a separate economic entity, they would constitute the 10th largest economy in the world with an economic buying power of about 3-4 trillion dollars.[22] But so much more remains to be done because their homes are not worth that much. And since slaves could not transfer their wealth to the next generation, then Blacks could not really be wealthy. Even many Black households don't have bank accounts or access to bank services.[23]

ALLEVIATING POVERTY IN MINORITY COMMUNITIES

What should be done to alleviate poverty, especially among American Negroes? Well, even though the next general election came and went, hardly anyone talks about possible compensation for the American Negroes' free labor that built the roads, hospitals, canals, dams and farms in this country. Slavery lasted for about 200 - 300 years and was followed by another 200 years of Jim Crow at the turn of the 21st century, and we are now facing the residue of this inferno.

So, it behooves Uncle Sam to compensate the real American 'Negroes' or the 'Negroes' whose ancestors were under bondage here the day after emancipation in 1864. This should be a limited compensation program, not reparations.

Under this definition of 'Negroes', Colin Powell, Eric Holder, and other contemporaries will not qualify for compensation because their parents came here after the 1920s or the 30s, and there is nothing to show that any of their parents were ever enslaved in America. But because of this group's high education they have more wealth than the slaves who came here under bondage before the Civil War. This group

22 https://www.newswise.com/articles/minority-markets-have-3-9-trillion-buying-power
23 See The Wall Street Journal, Sat-Sun, Nov. 7-8, 2020.

may oppose a Restitution Program, part of which is now under consideration at Georgetown University. No doubt a partial payment of wages due to the American Negro would improve contemporary living standards, and any residue transferred to the next generation would multiply wealth in the Black community. Certainly, it would reduce homelessness. As one can see, every social program since LBJ has been underfunded, and not much was accomplished for the Negro.

America has a lot of social problems which foreigners are not aware of until they come here, like the homeless can be found everywhere from D.C. to Los Angeles. This could be due to poor housing and economic blight where their salaries are below the minimum wage. Government figures show that 1 in 500 Americans is homeless. But as mentioned in Chapter 7, apart from San Francisco that spent $350 per year on the homeless in 2019, no other jurisdiction deploys resources of that scale, yet San Francisco's homeless group keeps growing.[24] But it appears the homeless don't have economic might to influence the government to enact policies that will benefit them.

Decent housing is also in short supply. A place like Baltimore has thousands of abandoned and substandard buildings. But because of politics, nothing gets done. The federal or state government should declare an emergency in Baltimore and decree that if one were to buy an abandoned building it should be improved and made livable within 3 years. Under the current scenario, the time limit is 6 months. It is impossible for a lot of first-time homeowners to comply, so they end up losing their properties to the government, or Baltimore sanctions them.

24 See The New Yorker, June 1, 2020, pp. 30-32.

In addition, the federal government should amend the tax code so that if a company like GM or GE were to procure some of its supplies from minority-owned businesses, the government automatically on tax day will give credit equal to the amount of its purchase to the bigger company, GE or GM. This incentive would encourage large companies to do business with small ones. At the moment, there is no such incentive, and many large companies are not eager to buy from small businesses. They think small businesses don't measure up to scale. The government should have ombudsmen in various parts of the country and if a citizen encounters a problem with a law enforcement agency or a big corporation like GE in a credit situation, the person can seek immediate resolution via an ombudsmen at virtually no cost. At the moment, litigation with a big company can be fatal to a small firm.

Another thing that will help minorities—whose communities are usually mass incarcerated—to live in this country peacefully is that after someone has served his prison sentence, the government should consider wiping his slate clean of any criminal record, especially if the ex-offender has served his sentence, probation, and paid his court fine in full. Then there should be no impediment like a criminal record to prohibit him from living anywhere he wants or pursuing any job he is qualified for. Under the current system, there is a large group of Blacks who can't get jobs anywhere because of their criminal records. In essence, they are permanently disenfranchised even though they are Americans.

As minorities, we shouldn't forget to be prompt, punctual, and reliable, for these are the characteristics needed to operate hospitals, schools and businesses in the White man's world. After all, as we learn how to drive cars, trucks, and aircrafts we are crossing over to the White man's world, and we should strive to acquire the characteristics required to operate successfully in this environment.

THE CHURCH IN THE BLACK AMERICAN COMMUNITY

One untapped source of strength and money is the Black Church. No one knows how many churches we have, but if all these churches combine their resources into a grand credit union Blacks, both native-born and foreign-born, could save and borrow money. We could then have the resources to buy and sell to each other goods and services like gas stations and supermarkets and finance our mortgages and student loans for our kids.

Some churches provide affordable housing for seniors. Others operate charter schools in big cities like New York and Washington, D.C. Now, since churches are non-profits, the government should encourage them to do what they do best which is, after all, act as a supplement to government social programs. Now, despite its enormous wealth, contemporary Black churches haven't done much for the poor in Black communities. Some have huge extravagant halls adjacent to their churches. But in the winter those halls are locked up and the homeless can't come in.

But the Methodist Church with White congregations where membership is declining because of age have started opening their doors mainly to Black males who can spend the night there. Another church that is doing similar pro bono services is the Lutheran Church opposite the Watergate Hotel in Washington, D.C. In addition to providing limited overnight housing, they give out free dinners to their clients who are mainly Black males. The Gonzaga School, a Jesuit High School also in D.C. has a large pantry that provides free lunches to many Black men.

Looking at every aspect of this Great Nation since the Reconstruction, American Blacks have been everywhere on the economic scale, in the Arts, Science, Sports, the Armed Forces, and the Presidency. But there is still work to be done since Jim Crow held Blacks back from transferring their families' wealth from one generation to the next.

But if Blacks continue with the gains they have made in colleges and universities in the last 50 years, we will one day see Black CEOs of Morgan and Chase Banks and on Wall Street. But what is never discussed in the Washington Post and the New York Times is the lack of cooperation among Blacks. To continue moving forward, we need to seal this leak.

Amazingly, why Blacks lag behind on the economic ladder is not mentioned by current popular books on the subject of economic disparity as propounded in 'Deaths of Despair and the Future of Capitalism' by authors Anne Case and Angus Deaton and other books. Summarily, the average White household's net worth is 70 cents to the dollar as opposed to Black's household net worth of 17 cents to the dollar. The key reason is that Whites even during Slavery in this country have been able to build their wealth when a father transfers wealth to his son, something Blacks lack. While Blacks are heavy consumers of food, cars and clothing, they have virtually no manufacturing plants that can hire workers and pay them good wages. So government distribution of income for the American Negro will be a good idea. But even if suggestions on closing the economic gap is mentioned, it is presented in the press as reparation or a mass give-away that will repel Whites from supporting such a program. That is why the American Negro should lobby for compensation for unpaid labor. And the American Negro is not someone who just landed here from Africa, but the survivors of Negroes that were brough to America as bondage. They are the ones through no fault of their own were left behind in higher education and getting ahead in America. Any program not tailored for this structure is bound to falter. Even President Lyndon B. Johnson's Great Society programs didn't make the distinction between the American Negro and foreign-born Blacks. So we took advantage of opportunities we did not deserve for none of my relatives was ever a slave in North America.

TAKING ANOTHER STAB AT RACISM

To restate, American Negroes in this context are the ancestors of the Blacks brought over from Africa or any Black in America on the day the Civil War ended. This will be a limited compensation for unpaid labor, not reparations. I believe White America will accept this proposal.

Other efforts to bridge the economic gap should include the federal government's attempt to recover the assets of Blacks that Whites stole during the Reconstruction. In 2017, a Harvard Professor recounted a story of a Black woman who owned over a thousand acres of land in North Carolina. Somehow this land owner was tardy to pay the property tax of only $300 in the 1940s. Despite her legitimate excuse of the lapse, the State of North Carolina sold the entire lot of 1,600 acres for pennies and gave the property to a White family.

Now, since North Carolina couldn't do anything for this woman, Uncle Sam should pay a nominal sum to the survivors of the landlady. Through these schemes, the American Negro could make partial recoveries of lost assets or wealth.

Now, from what we know now, Trump wasn't the ideal President to ask to consider compensating Blacks for losses, for he repeatedly, according to the Carpenter's Union, did stiff his contractors who came to work for him in Atlantic City. But Mr. and Mrs. Clinton, Obama, and Biden had no excuse not to apply executive fiats to compensate Blacks in a way that would restore parity in wealth today between Whites and non-Whites. To Biden such an action will look bewildering for by nature he is nonconfrontational. Summarily, the President should issue an Executive fiat to compensate the survivors of the Negroes who were here the day the Civil War ended. Obama could have issued such a fiat to cut a check for deserving Blacks. Apparently, he had no interest to help his fellow Blacks apart from giving them food stamps. This isn't a reparation, but rather it should be regarded as a limited form of compensation. Georgetown University is working on a similar plan.

As mentioned, under this deal, Blacks like Colin Powell, Eric Holder, and some others will be excluded from such a compensation program. This is because their parents came to the US from the Caribbean in the 1920s and 1930s, and there is no evidence that they were enslaved here. Also excluded would be Blacks whose ancestors came here from Panama, Jamaica, and elsewhere but were never enslaved in America.

Some may say that even though I am foreign-born, and I got ripped off by American lawyers and judges, I was able to overcome my difficulties. Well, yes, this is only partly true in the sense that I have been able to acquire 4–5 college degrees in the US and by the age of 50 was a millionaire.

BEWARE OF THE FALLACY OF BIG NAMES

There are some in the US who portray themselves as people who fight for the Little Guy. Obviously, individuals like Oprah Winfrey, Ellen DeGeneres, and Chef José Andres have been kind to a lot of people without asking for anything in return. But there are others who are walking around telling the world that they are friends of the Little Guy, but actually are not.

For example, as mentioned earlier when Judge Messitte and his friends stole our assets, I wrote President Obama, his wife, and his mother-in-law, but they all turned their backs on me. Later, I did learn Obama was friends with Prosecutor Rosenstein because they had gone to Harvard Law School together. Professor Alan Dershowitz, a Harvard Professor was the same. He fights only for Jews. In other words, Obama's friendship with Rosenstein was more important than my predicament, which shouldn't have been because I am like Obama's father who went to a foreign country to seek his fortune. So, I thought Obama being the President and in charge of the Executive Branch could have asked the Justice Department to look into my case for wrongdoing, if any.

Chapter 11

Some of the Famous and Near Famous I Have Met or Corresponded with In My Lifetime

While I was growing up in Ghana in the 60s, I had the fortune of meeting important people. Among them were Emperor Haile Selassie, the ruler of Ethiopia at that time; Queen Elizabeth II, when she came to Ghana to celebrate Ghana's independence; and the then president of Ghana, Kwame Nkrumah. Even I was looking forward to meeting Patrice Lumumba, the President of the Congo at that time, but he never made it to Ghana because the rebels in his country killed him. I had two rich grand uncles who took me around state and football functions, and in the process I met some VIPs.

This luck of meeting or corresponding with important people continued when I came to the United States. My

German boss' wife, after giving me several books to read to kill the time suggested I should write some of the authors whose books I had read or were about to read. So, I asked her what I should write about and she suggested I should give my impressions of their books. She also said I should not ask for money or anything else.

So, that is how for a brief time I exchanged letters with Justice William O. Douglas, once a Supreme Court Justice. But then he fell ill, and the letters dried up. Then there was Ted Kennedy the Senator from Massachusetts with whom I tried to communicate with briefly. I wrote about his brother Joseph who died during World War II and JFK who sought to extend America's worldwide influence through the Peace Corps. I had been taught by the Peace Corps. He really did like that, and later he gave me my first job with the US government. Then there was my pen pal Mr. Donald Graham, the ex-publisher of the Washington Post. During a 10-year period, we exchanged lots of letters, but when I told him Judge Messitte had stolen our assets, Mr. Graham stopped writing me. Later on, I learned that he and his family knew Messitte. Even though Messitte now lives in Montgomery County, he was born in Washington and so was Mr. Graham, so Graham was making a choice between his homeboy and me, the damn foreigner. There are others, but they are too numerous to mention here.

I still read voraciously. Once when I was in government detention for about 6 months I read close to 200 books. Upon my return, I continued reading, namely magazines such as Harper, Rolling Stone, Harvard Business Review, The Nation, Vanity, Psychology Today, Contemporary American Political Issues, The Atlantic, The Economist, and numerous others. I also read The Washington Post,

The New York Times, Financial Times of London, The Wall Street Journal, and The Sun daily to expand my knowledge. But I don't think my knowledge should be concentrated in English only. So, I have taught myself Spanish, German, Italian, Portuguese, French and Akan.

All this has expanded my horizons and influenced my ability to correspond with all kinds of people, from college professors to truck drivers.

It is God's blessing that I met some important people in Ghana and elsewhere. Among these blessings is corresponding was the Senior George Bush, the President who helped to sponsor some of my siblings here.

Also, I do recall when I was 10 years old the whole school was let out to stand on the sidewalk to see W.E.B. Dubois passing by. This was around 1960. If anyone had told you this was a Black man you would not have believed it. He appeared white and wore a white shirt, and the sun was shining that hour so I couldn't see him well. All I saw of him were his little hands waving to the crowd.

The other person I met when I was young was Haile Selassie of Ethiopia. We all wanted to see him because it was rumored that he had a lion and we, as kids, wanted to see it.

At Ghana's Independence in 1957, Queen Elizabeth II came to represent the United Kingdom at a celebration. At that time, she was young and very beautiful. In fact, she still looks like my cousin Tina.

Among other VIPs I have come into contact with in my lifetime were Mr. Donald Graham and his mother,

Katherine Graham, of the Washington Post newspaper. One thing unusual is that I have never personally met them, but we were pen pals. Mr. Graham liked my critical thinking when I showed him my various writings on social and political issues like the Palestinian conflict and social issues in the US. Mr. Graham sounded intelligent, and I expected advanced thoughts from him. But later on, he appeared to be like anybody else with 5 grandchildren and divorced.

Another famous person I ran into by accident was Cesar Chavez, a union organizer who tried to win good working conditions and wages for Hispanic and immigrant laborers. He was so powerful some thought he might run for a high office in California, but he never did. I met him one night at Clark University campus in Worcester, Massachusetts. Upon closer view, he was just an ordinary looking man.

But there were others I was fortunate to have met, namely Kwame Nkrumah, first President of Ghana and his spouse Fathia; Cab Calloway, the entertainer; Arthur Mitchell of the Dance Theater of Harlem; John H. Johnson, Publisher of Ebony magazine; and Senator Edward Brooke, a Black politician from Massachusetts who did help with my siblings' visas. Gene Molovinsky, my Jewish insurer, is a kind person. Out there in Temple Hills, Maryland, he runs a camp for Black males without fathers to train them in boxing. He has produced several champions, even some at the national level. But Molovinsky is so humble he doesn't take credit for his achievement.

One characteristic about remarkable people is you may be more likely to get a response from that person if one does a study about what interests them the most. In my case, I had some common characteristics with Justice William O.

Douglas that formed a connection. For example, my father died early and Douglas' father died early, too, and both our mothers on their limited resources struggled to give us the best education. So, one has to get a common affinity to such a busy person to write you back because they don't always have time to chit chat.

Another remarkable thing I noticed about these great people is that it is difficult to look them in the eye when one meets them.

The Great and Famous Who Corresponded With Or Met David Kissi

	Person	Period
1	Dr. E.B. Dubois, a Negro Political Activist	Met in Ghana in the mid-60s
2	Emperor Haile Selassie – Lion of Juda, Ethiopian Ruler	Met in Ghana in the mid-60s
3	Queen Elizabeth II of Great Britain	Met in Ghana in 1957
4	Kwame Nkrumah, 1st President of Ghana	Met in Ghana in the mid-60s
5	Supreme Court Justice William O. Douglas	Wrote each other in the early 1970s
6	Ted Kennedy, US Senator from Massachusetts	Found DK his first government job in the 1970s
7	John Kenneth Galbraith, Economic Advisor to President Kennedy, Canadian by birth	Correspondence
8	Cesar Chavez, the Mexican-American union organizer	Met at Clark University in 1976
9	George Bush Sr., President, USA 1980s	Helped with siblings' visas
10	Nancy Reagan, President Ronald Reagan's wife	1980s – was helpful
11	Senator Edward Brooks of Massachusetts	1980s constituent matters

12	Donald Graham, ex-Publisher of the Wash Post	A pen pal then
13	Katherine Graham, Donald's mother and former Owner of the Washington Post	A review of Ms. Graham's autobiography-'A Personal Journey'
14	Marion Barry, ex-Mayor of DC	Astute Politician
15	Parren Mitchell, US Congressman from Baltimore	Constituent matters in the 1990s
16	Van Braun, ex-German Chancellor, died in the mid-80s, Berlin	World Affairs in the 1990s
17	John H. Johnson, Owner of Ebony and Jet magazines	Black History in the 1990s
18	Lee Iaccoca, Chairman of Ford Motor Co.	Sought Iaccoca's advice in 2007 and 2009. His website invited people to write him and share their experiences after he retired from Chrysler.
19	Cab Calloway, A Black Entertainer	DC Warner Theater
20	Arthur Mitchell, Founder of Dance Theater of Harlem	Met at the Kennedy Center, DC in 1990
21	Nana Joseph Adomako, DK's benefactor	1960 - 1970
22	Mike Miller, Maryland State Senator, Annapolis General Assembly	2018 - 2020
23	Kofi Annan, for UN Secretary General	Met him at Houston Hall, Howard University in 1995

NB: *One useful lesson in dealing with the above is not to ask for monetary assistance, but you could ask for a job or legal assistance. And the best advice in getting someone to write you back is to raise issues that concern their interest. For example, when I wrote Justice Douglas I did let him know his mother, like my mother, was a widow who did all that she could to get the best education for her children. Later, we named our company Yakima Paper Supplies after Yakima, Washington in honor of Justice Douglas who grew up there.*

Chapter 12

A Summary of the Last 50 Years

I have not been to Ghana in about 50 years. The reason is that I spent about 20 years arguing over $2 million worth of assets. Then I had to spend another 20 years to try to recover it from Emil Hirsch, evil lawyers, and the US government. I am like modern-day Maria Altmann, the Jewish woman who successfully spent 60 years battling the Austrian government to get back her grandfather's art collection. Eventually she succeeded.

Subconsciously, I would not like to return to Ghana. For the New York Times and the Financial Times both report that Ghana today is much poorer compared with its post-Independence economy. I would rather prefer to retire to Switzerland, a place I immensely admire from my last visit. They have their own problems but not on a large scale as in America.

Chapter 13

Looking Back! Would I Do It All Over Again? 'Yes or No'

A "Yes" or "No" response would not necessarily reflect failure or absolute success, and I am just grateful for all the opportunities the US has given me. After all, I accomplished a lot on both my mother's and my own agenda acquiring post-graduate school degrees in Business and Economics. In addition, I became a millionaire at age 50, went to Europe twice, and sponsored 20 individuals including relatives, their siblings, and schoolmates from Ghana and Nigeria to the United States.

Also, in the US I did learn how to sail and swim. I also took classes on how to use an iPad. Until the pandemic came to town, I used to attend church twice a week at St. Matthews in D.C. I also once became a teacher's assistant at its International Language School in D.C. Every day I meet interesting people from all over the world when I am on the road or making sales calls. I do agree without doubt that I am a good and a forceful salesman. This has been my secret weapon to becoming successful. I have also acquired the ability to befriend and influence people. All this has helped me to stay in business for about 38 years.

But if I were to begin all over again, I would have settled in Switzerland at an early age because Blacks are treated better.

On the other hand, if I had chosen to stay in Ghana right after secondary school at the ages of 15 to 18, I and my brothers could have expanded our family cocoa farm to about 1,000 acres, and it could have yielded substantial sums for the extended family to have built a nest egg for retirement and the future generation. But I would have died early as my contemporaries in Ghana died prematurely from prostate cancer, colon cancer, high blood pressure, and heart attacks. These are ailments for which the African Juju man has no answers.

Also, in looking back I am becoming more aware of some of the puzzles of American society, for example, if I had started out as a UPS driver making $25 per hour while enrolled at a community college with a small mortgage and two kids at University of Maryland, it's likely Judge Messitte would not have come after me for anything for he may presume I do not have substantial assets. And apart from getting a traffic ticket it's unlikely I would have met the police anywhere.

But in any case, at the age of 50 we had 16 properties, and I and my wife were millionaires. And that is where the American system gets ugly. With no standing, one Emil Hirsch, a debt collector working in collusion with Judge Messitte placed restraining orders and injunctions that caused us to lose our assets. At that point, White males we had gotten to know for a long time sought to avoid us because of the mixture of our money and misfortune. And that is how a White American helps his fellow White to commit crimes – with his silence. We quickly learned that a non-White foreigner would in all likelihood become a target of the FBI and US Prosecutors, turncoat lawyers, and judges if there is a substantial amount of money in a litigation. The America White man is more likely to call for reinforcement from law enforcement agencies to help him collect and even liquidate a foreign-born person's assets under false pretexts. It doesn't even matter if the victim, like in my case, is threatened with deportation to finally silence him. Perhaps to avoid too much exposure, many foreigners, especially Hispanics and Asians, purposely sound semi-illiterate and they live in their own little enclaves to preserve their wealth and later go back to their countries of origin.

All this may sound like a contradiction to one's goal of coming to America and getting ahead. But the reality is different, especially for the ones who don't know the real America.

Chapter 14

Conclusion

There has been a shift in the center of power in the US for the last 40 years and that shift has evolved from an informal transfer of power from Congress to some group of non-elected persons. Since these individuals are not elected by the people, they are not responsive to the rights of the masses. This group consists mainly of retired military officers, business executives, judges, and US prosecutors. And they do the good and bad jobs that Congress or the Executive Branch don't want to touch.

In modern times, former Governor Richardson of New Mexico, on two occasions, went to North Korea to rescue two Americans under detention in that country. And former President Jimmy Carter, after he left office, went to North Korea for the same purpose. All these were operating informally without Congressional authority.

Ronald Reagan allegedly sent intermediaries in 1980 in Iran to urge the Ayatollah not to release American hostages until he became President, but this was in contradiction to the then US policy to bring the hostages home. This informal resolution while convenient may have saved the President's face if something had gone awry, could also have led to miscommunications at a high level of government.

There are other informal groups operating outside Congress. Among them are R.J. Rosenstein, a federal prosecutor in Maryland. Rosenstein is known to recommend stiff sentences for the least possession of crack and on some occasions he can round-up 50 to 100 gun and drug offenders in one single swoop. Almost all will be Black men. Most could be beneficiaries of government job training programs but are lost through Rosenstein's swoops. This partly explains why jobs and housing suffer in Baltimore.

Now, some people blame Mr. Biden for sponsoring the anti-crack legislation in Congress, but he is a decent man such that he may not urge a judge to impose a 50-year sentence on a defendant for possessing a few grams of a drug, but Rosenstein will. Ironically, this same defendant we are talking about here in Swedish court would have gotten only 6 months of home confinement in Sweden. But if America's criminal justice system's intent is to rehabilitate criminal defendants, then our system is clearly not working because of long sentences and repeat offenders that have contributed to build up a large pool of poor Blacks. Rosenstein's associates who are also working under the second-tier class of the new power structure are Michael Schatzow, a former US Prosecutor; Merrick Garland, Head of the current US Department of Justice; Judge Peter J. Messitte and former Judge Alexander Williams – both of Maryland; Judge Goodwin of West Virginia and the Martin O'Malley, former Governor of Maryland. All these people, not the Chinese, threaten the Foundation of the Republic.

This new class of rulers or second-tier group of rulers are so powerful they can influence who should be the mayor in a jurisdiction like D.C. and give free passes to big banks, social media, and trading firms like Amazon and Walmart. In fact, Joe Biden cannot do anything about this new development and that is why when one writes him about the second tier of government, he doesn't know what to say. He is no R.F. Kennedy so, the bad guys under the guise of the government keep winning and undermine security here and abroad.

Another development that has undermined us is the weakening of the average person's relationship with the Federal Government. Now, when the average adult hears from the government, he is terrified, i.e., the IRS, DEA, and the FBI. But I recall there was a time as recently as 30 years ago when one could freely visit and roam through the Pentagon and the GSA building unimpeded. In those days, the Pentagon and the GSA were under instructions from President Reagan to buy whatever they need from small and minority businesses before procurement solicits prices from General Electric, General Motors, Ford, etc. But today virtually all US government agencies from the US Department of Labor to the GSA have closed their doors to the Little Guy. This overall weakens the interaction of the Citizen and his Government. Now, if the Citizen doesn't know what is happening behind the closed doors of the government and it appears his input to government decision-making is now disregarded even though he is a taxpayer, then that makes him a second-class citizen too. This is the America even people born here don't even know. And since conversely, the government doesn't offhand know what people are doing on the street, government resorts to remote monitoring and spying on its own people. (See NY Times 4/2021, a federal judge's rebuke of Uncle Sam in this regard.) This has made some Americans unhappy and non-trusting of government.

Perhaps citizens' discontent and denial of their liberal access to the courts and the misconduct of Rosenstein et al poses more of a threat to America's Foundation than what the Chinese economy might do to us, or that a resurgent Japan is capable of 'getting even' over Pearl Harbor. This nation should remove the speck from its eyes before we suggest others do the same for it will help us to identify what our problems are and how to resolve them well. No doubt it is wise to have a transparent form of government with citizens' access to the main buildings guaranteed. All this will rather make us stronger to counter our foreign enemies. And attempts to undermine the Republic as nearly happened on January 6, 2021, will be diminished.

At the end I figured if there are a lot of bad things in the US, it's my duty, too, to try and help fix some of the issues after America tried to help me. So, I adapted and became a benefactor and yearly sent cash to schools, colleges, and institutions. Among them are:

- Husson University
- Boston College
- Northeastern University
- Worcester State University
- Holy Cross College
- Clark University
- University of Maryland, College Park
- University of Maryland Medical School
- George Washington University

- The Shriners
- International Fellowship of Christians and Jews
- Wounded Warriors
- Paralyzed Veterans
- The Salvation Army
- A Girls School in Afghanistan
- Then there was a group of girls in Balizenda, Ethiopia where USAID assisted us to distribute money and hygiene products. In fact, in this instance my wife did pay off the bondage debt of a young Ethiopian girl who wasn't able to go to school because she had to work for another family to pay off the debt her family owed them.
- Worcester Polytechnical Institute
- Boys Town in Nebraska
- St. Joseph's Lakota Indian School in South Dakota
- St. Ignatius School for Boys, Baltimore, MD
- Before my sister Regina died in 2007 she suggested I should send her Kwabeya School pens, pencils, and notepads to the students. In response, I donated about a thousand pens and pencils.
- From 2000 – 2020 book packages sent to the wardens at various prisons:
  - FCI Danbury, CT
  - CI NE Ohio Correctional Center, Youngstown, OH
  - FCI Cumberland, MD
  - Maryland Correctional Institution for Women Jessup, MD
  - DOC, Baltimore, MD
  - FCI Beckley, Beaver, WV
  - DC Jail, Washington, DC
  - Baltimore Pre-Release Unit for Women, Baltimore

- Metropolitan Correctional Center, NY, NY
- Alternative and Special Detention, Philadelphia, PA
- Loudoun County Detention Center, Leesburg, VA
- Cook County Dept. of Corrections, Chicago, IL
- Pitchess Detention Center-East Facility, Castaic, CA
- Alternative and Special Detention, Philadelphia, PA
- Fairfax Detention Center, Fairfax, VA

As the record shows, the extent of my giveaway in the beginning was to help individuals to come to this country or get medical assistance when on their own they could not afford it. But I changed track about 10 years ago so that the general public can benefit, too.

A case in point was when about three years ago I recruited the D.C. Council Representative for Ward 3 to help rehab the US Postal Service Building in Cleveland Park, a suburb of Washington, D.C., when that building had fallen into disrepair. Furthermore, I launched a mail campaign to convince some members of Congress to provide funds for the rehab of the building. The end result was a successful completion of a building made new. And today individuals on Connecticut Ave. and Ordway in Cleveland Park in D.C. have a wonderful post office.

I inherited this trait from my mother who was considered a Saint. She was so kind that she helped her siblings and neighbors all the time. For example, in one instance she helped a friend of mine whose parents didn't have the money to send him to a missionary-run school, back when the British ran the schools. My mother resolved this problem by talking to the school principal to waive this friend's tuition. Years later, as I understand it, this guy became a famous mathematician in Ghana, but my mother never took credit for it.

Similarly, I have done a lot to help my brothers and sisters, widows, and others. As recently as 3 or 4 years ago, the Reverend Walter Fauntroy, a former Associate of Civil Rights Leader, Martin Luther King, Jr. got immersed in a business deal with a vicious woman who nearly had him locked up for bouncing a check. When a friend of mine sought my help in this matter, I agreed to raise about $22,000 for Reverend Fauntroy to pay off his creditor and place a note on his home that was at risk of foreclosure. When this matter was finally resolved, the Reverend Fauntroy forgot all about the foot soldiers like me who went the extra mile to rescue him from jail.

And there was an Ethiopian friend of mine, Anafi, who was half blind. Since he could not afford a medical bill of $9,100, I took him to Dr. Ashburn in McLean, Virginia. The doctor fixed his eyes for him at no cost. These are the things I do that make me happy. And I inherited this sense of helping others all from my mother. In addition, my wife, too, has helped so many people without looking for anything in return. But I think the most effective way to help people is not to give the store away, but rather to help them help themselves.

To round up this great story; I will assert that I have learned so much, not only about myself and other Blacks but from the American Negro too, and also about this country overall , and I am grateful for that.

David Kissi, Author, age 72

Thank You

Thank You For Reading My Book!

I really appreciate all of your feedback, and I love hearing what you have to say.

I need your input to make the next version of this book and my future books even better.

Please leave me a helpful review on Amazon letting me know what you thought of the book.

Thank you so much!
David Kissi

About Happy Self Publishing

Happy Self Publishing is a one-stop destination for online publishing services such as book cover design, editing, formatting, audiobook narration, website design,and marketing. At Happy Self Publishing we help authors find their voice and self-publish professionally.

▶ **WHAT WE DO:** We help coaches, consultants, trainers, speakers, and entrepreneurs who aspire to position themselves as the trusted experts in their field by helping them become bestselling authors within 6 months or less, even if they hate writing.

▶**HOW WE DO IT:** We show you how to build a profitable author funnel and use the book as the lead magnet in the funnel to give you expert positioning and attract qualified leads for your business.

▶**WHY IT WORKS:** After working with over 400 authors from 35 countries, we've been able to simplify the process and show you the easiest and fastest way to publish your book. It doesn't matter at what stage of your author journey you are currently - we have the tools & resources to take you to the next step and help you publish a world-class book.

▶**SERVICES WE PROVIDE:**
✓ book writing aka angel writing
✓ editing
✓ book coaching
✓ book cover design
✓ formatting
✓ publishing ebooks, paperback & audiobooks
✓ author websites
✓ book trailers
✓ making it a #1 Amazon bestseller

Check us out on www.happyselfpublishing.com
YouTube: www.youtube.com/jyotsnaramachandran
Instagram: www.instagram.com/happyselfpub/
LinkedIn: www.linkedin.com/company/happyselfpublishing/mycompany/
Join our Happy Authors' Tribe:
www.facebook.com/groups/happyauthorstribe

Made in the USA
Columbia, SC
14 October 2021

46839884R00081